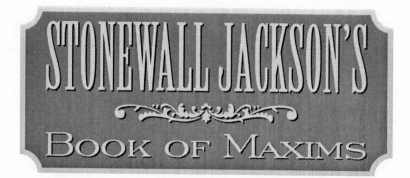

STONEWALL JACKSON'S
BOOK OF MAXIMS

Edited by

JAMES I. ROBERTSON JR.

CUMBERLAND HOUSE

AN IMPRINT OF SOURCEBOOKS, INC.

STONEWALL JACKSON'S BOOK OF MAXIMS
PUBLISHED BY CUMBERLAND HOUSE PUBLISHING, AN IMPRINT OF SOURCEBOOKS, INC.
  P.O. Box 4410
  Naperville, IL 60567-4410
  www.sourcebooks.com

All Scripture quotations are taken from the King James Version.

Cover design by Gore Studio, Nashville, Tennessee.

Library of Congress Cataloging-in-Publication Data

Jackson, Stonewall, 1824–1863.
    Stonewall Jackson's book of maxims / edited by James I. Robertson, Jr.
       p.   cm.
    Includes bibliographical references and index.
     1. Jackson, Stonewall, 1824–1863—Quotations. 2. Generals—Confederate States of America—Quotations. 3. Conduct of life—Quotations, maxims, etc. I. Robertson, James I. II. Title.
    E467.1.J15 J17 2002
    973.7'3'092—dc21

                                     2002005876

Printed in the United States of America.

RRD 10 9 8 7 6 5 4 3

When wisdom entereth into thine heart,
and knowledge is pleasant unto thy soul;
Discretion shall preserve thee,
understanding shall keep thee. . . .

Trust in the LORD with all thine heart;
and lean not unto thine own understanding.
In all thy ways acknowledge him,
and he shall direct thy paths.

—*Proverbs* 2:10–11; 3:5–6

CONTENTS

INTRODUCTION

FEW MEN HAVE EVER started from humbler beginnings and risen to greater heights. He never sought fame, but he could not escape its light when opportunity came. The louder people cheered, the more embarrassed he became. He was fatally wounded by "friendly fire" in 1863; writers of every generation since have asserted that had he lived, the Confederate States of America might have triumphed.

Such was Gen. Thomas Jonathan Jackson, whose sobriquet "Stonewall" remains the most famous nickname in American military history.

One Virginia veteran stated of Jackson: "Of all the generals on the side of the South, he, and he alone, infused into the minds of the rank and file of the army unquestioning confidence and utter reliance. . . . No other general could get from the soldiers what Stonewall Jackson secured without an effort. The privates of the army adored him; and no matter whether the ground was covered with snow, or rain poured in blinding torrents, or the sun beat with vivid force upon the heads and their feet sunk in the dust a foot deep, they would follow the old tattered uniform, that old faded gray hat, that kindly, rugged face, until nature itself would rebel."[1]

Another Confederate put it more simply: "There was something about Jackson that always attracted his men. It must have been faith. . . . The very sight of him was the signal for cheers."[2]

In 1862 an Englishman declared for the ages: "If the South had done nothing more in this revolution than to give the world such a character as Jackson, she would need no further vindication in her noble struggle for independence."[3]

Before he became one of the greatest field commanders of all time, Jackson traveled on an oftentimes lonely and rocky highway of life. His Jackson forebears had been prominent settlers in the mountainous wilderness of northwestern Virginia. Yet by the time of Tom Jackson's birth in 1824, his branch of the family had fallen not only on hard times but some public scandal as well.

He was only two when his father died. When Tom was seven, his mother was forced to give him and a young sister to other family members. The boy grew up on the prosperous farm of an uncle crude and roughhewn in every approach to life save greed. Cummins Jackson gave his nephew a sense of security, little opportunities for education, and even less of love.

Loneliness and solitude were the lad's closest companions through the formative years. The result was a boy who was shy, withdrawn, reticent. In many ways Tom Jackson was never a child; in many ways he was also the little unloved boy whose only defense in later life was to avoid close relationships that might cause him further unhappiness.

The labor of his life was to make himself more than a farmer in the mountainous country of northwestern Virginia. A desire for knowledge was the one passion of his youth, Jackson's wife Anna later noted. "With the pride of descent from a family that had stood high in the country round, he felt deeply the disadvantages which his early orphanage and poverty had entailed upon him, and was ambitious to make a position for himself, and keep up the prestige of his name."[4]

At the age of eighteen, almost by default, Jackson secured an appointment to the U.S. Military Academy.[5] He was poorly prepared for the academic demands of what was then the finest engineering school in America. Jackson, however, was aware that West Point was likely the only chance he was going to have to make any significant achievement in his life. He was determined to battle every obstacle, overcome every impediment, to attain his goal of graduation.

Plebes trying to adjust to a military life grew weary of hearing endless pontifications from commandant of cadets J. Addison Thomas. Yet as the fourth classmen were about to move into their barracks, Jackson surely took to heart Captain Thomas's exhortation: "You are not common soldiers! You are Gentlemen—Gentlemen of manners, of politeness, and of education! The United States looks to you! The Country looks to you!"[6]

Studies came hard to the poorly educated orphan. So did friends. John C. Tidball, a year behind Jackson at West Point, remembered the Virginian well. "In consequence of a somewhat shambling, awkward gait, and the habit of carrying his head down in a thoughtful attitude, he seemed less of stature than he really was. His features, without being homely, were rather strongly marked. He had bluish gray eyes and a somewhat sallow complexion, but which inclined to ruddiness upon exercise or from blushing, a habit he was much given to from excessive diffidence. His nose, long and thin, and his forehead, broad and angular, were his most characteristic features. Being an intense student, his mind appeared to be constantly preoccupied, and he seldom spoke to anyone unless spoken to, and then his face lighted up blushingly, as that of a bashful person when complimented. His voice was thin and feminine—almost squeaky—while his utterances were quick, jerky and sententious, but when once made were there ended; there was no repetition or amending; no hypothesis or observation to lead to further discussion. When a jocular remark occurred in his hearing he smiled as though he understood and enjoyed it, but never ventured comment to promote further mirth."[7]

Jackson's four years at the academy consisted almost solely of study and solitary walks. Perseverance brought success. By sheer determination, Jackson rose from dead-last among the plebes in 1842 to seventeenth of fifty-nine graduates in the Class of 1846.

Few cadets in West Point history have ever matched such a climb up the academic ladder. Jackson's achievement was a fulfillment of the most famous of his maxims: "You may be what ever you will resolve to be."

During his years at West Point, Jackson received indoctrination into the basic social graces. He learned cleanliness and how to dress, how to keep one's hair combed and fingernails clean, how to bow, basic table manners, and the like. Certainly the unpolished mountain boy who arrived in 1842 was far removed from the officer and gentleman who departed West Point in 1846.

Heroism in the Mexican War brought three brevet promotions, recognition in the army, and the knowledge that the military was his true calling. For the next four years, Jackson shuttled among army posts. His duties were never more exciting than sitting on courts-martial. It was during this period that Jackson began a campaign of self-improvement. His career was seemingly established, but he still had a long way to overcome awkwardness, ignorance of the rules of society, and an all but total inability to engage in conversation. His new goal was to make his life more orderly and enjoyable.

"I thought at one time of writing a journal but I can not find the time," Jackson wrote his sister, Laura, in the spring of 1848. "My studies are now principally directed to the formation of my manners and the rules of society and a more thorough knowledge of human nature."[8]

For most of that postwar inactive time, Jackson was stationed at Fort Hamilton at the entrance to the harbor of New

York City. The hero was still a young officer who was awkward, friendless, and lonely. Yet Jackson was unconquerable.
He determined to undertake a thoroughgoing effort at making
his life as orderly as his military career. Jackson would continue
to be absolutely truthful, punctual, and as polite as he knew
how to be. At the same time, he sought knowledge, wanted to
find precise meaning in everything written or spoken, and
would work unceasingly to improve his spelling and grammar.

Among his first steps were regular visits to New York book-
stores. Jackson was not interested merely in acquiring a library.
He wanted to read in order to expand both his knowledge and
his behavioral patterns. Lord Chesterfield, the author who
would become his greatest guide, encouraged reading as the
means of "improving and refining style upon the best models.
. . . If you set out upon this principle, and keep it constantly in
your mind, every company you go into, and every book you
read, will contribute to your improvement, either by shewing
you what to imitate, or what to avoid." While books pointed out
"the operation of the mind, the sentiments of the heart, the influence of the passion," they were ineffectual "without subsequent
practice, experience, and observation."[9]

Jackson purchased volumes on a wide range of topics. From
the days he first learned to read, he had an abiding interest in
history. Jackson later would endorse this observation by Lord
Chesterfield: "By the help of history, a young man may, in some
measure, acquire the experience of old age. In reading what has
been done, he is apprised of what he has to do; the more he is
informed of what is past, the better he will know how to conduct himself for the future."[10]

His first purchases in New York treated of history, military
campaigns and biographies, government, ethics, and philosophy. In the winter of 1849, he told the congressman who had
appointed him to West Point: "I propose with the blessing of
Providence to be a hard student, and to make myself not only

acquainted with military art and science but with politics, and of course must be well versed in history. My historical studies I have aranged [sic] in the following order: first of general history, ancient and modern, and then, special histories of important events, countries, &c."[11]

By the following year, Jackson could exclaim to his sister: "It is probable that I am more particular in my rules than any person of your acquaintance."[12] This statement was indicative of the man. The determination that Jackson applied to every endeavor required planning. Hence, as he strove to improve his mind and his conduct, he was unbending in his efforts and inflexible in his approach.

Every word written or spoken was carefully chosen. Jackson labored diligently to avoid errors in grammar and spelling. He subscribed to the old principle that one should write "in the plain and simple language which is so obviously required in works which aim at permanent and practical usefulness."[13]

Good etiquette became for him as rigorous a pursuit as a military objective. He would not break rules. As one writer concluded, "In all aspects of his life Jackson wanted never to make a mistake."[14]

His book of maxims first appeared at this time. The 8⅛" x 10¼" blue-marbled notebook began as a list of criteria in choosing one's friends. From the start, the notebook was a reminder for self-improvement. Jackson began writing in the journal around 1848 and added statements over the next five years. The maxims were not strikingly original, as will be seen, nor were they always profound. They were simply intended to assist a timid, socially untutored young man in mastering the challenges of daily life in a learned society.

Those challenges became acute in 1851, when the twenty-seven-year-old Jackson left the army to become professor of natural and experimental philosophy at the Virginia Military Institute in Lexington. The school, only twelve years old, was growing steadily. Jackson had no experience as a college professor; he knew precious little about the subject matter he was to teach.[15] Nevertheless, he came to believe the precept that "teaching is ennobled by the great fact that God is a teacher."[16] Jackson again applied that strong focus and unbendable determination to his new tasks.

He never became an outstanding success in the classroom. A member of the VMI Board of Visitors spoke for many when he stated: "The impression he produced upon me was that he was a man of peculiarities, distinctly marked from the ordinary man of note, reserved yet polite, reticent of opinion, but fixed in the ideas he had formed, sensitively averse to obtruding them upon others, but determined and inflexible in their advocacy. . . . [His] abrupt manner and a crisp but not brusque form of expression did not tend to render him popular with the young men under his charge."[17]

An equal struggle Jackson had to wage in 1851–52 was Lexington society. The town might have seemed isolated at the southern end of the Shenandoah Valley and with the Blue Ridge Mountains separating it physically from the eastern "learned half" of the state. Residents of the town that boasted Washington College as well as VMI, however, were extremely urbane and intelligent. One citizen noted: "Apart from the professors' families, others, attracted by these opportunities of education, have made Lexington their home; so that it has become known in all the country not only as a seat of learning, but of general cultivation, refinement, and hospitality."[18]

Into this environment stepped Jackson. He made a generally unfavorable first impression. VMI professor Raleigh Colston said of his new colleague: "Somewhat above middle height, his figure was large-boned, angular and even ungainly for his hands & especially his feet were very large. . . . He wore at that time the old style military side-whiskers 'not lower than the corner of the mouth' as prescribed by army regulations. This gave to his countenance a stiff and formal expression which his conversation by no means tended to remove, for he had but little to say, spoke in brief sentences & curt tones & was somewhat constrained in his manners, as was natural with one who had mingled but little in general society."

James Power Smith, later one of Jackson's strongest admirers, observed that "the Major" (as most Lexingtonians at first labeled Jackson) "was abrupt in speech and manner, sometimes absentminded and aloof, and not interested in many things that interested others, and somewhat peculiar in his gait and gestures."[19]

At that time the Reverend Dr. George Junkin was president of Washington College. This future father-in-law of Jackson had just published a small work with thoughts that certainly inspired "the new man on the block." Junkin stated: "The fields of exertion are no longer closed against the sons of poverty and humble birth. . . . The arena for magnificent achievement is free to all; and in the glorious rivalry for intellectual superiority, class is not arrayed against class, but all are welcomed to a generous equality."[20]

Jackson's entrance into Lexington society was slow, exceedingly painful, but eventually successful. That he paid heed to the maxims he developed and recorded is obvious.

His first friend in town was John B. Lyle, a courteous, jolly, and lovable old bachelor who ran a bookstore on Main Street. Lyle was an alumnus of Washington College and a kinsman of many of the leading citizens of both the town and Rockbridge County. He did more than introduce Jackson to the world of literature; Lyle also guided him into the hierarchy of local society. His bookstore, wrote one browser, "had become a sort of clubhouse in which assembled frequently the professional men of the town, the professors and officers of the College and Institute, and every genteel young man of the community."[21]

Jackson called these acquaintances "the kind of friends with whom I feel at home." They counseled him informally and personally on many matters, Jackson added, "without the marred pleasure resulting from a conviction that afterwards all my conduct must undergo a judicial investigation before 'Judge Etiquette.'"[22]

Not a naturally social man, Jackson at first attended Lexington soirees more from a sense of duty than from desire. Young Clement Fishburne met Jackson on several of these occasions. Jackson, Fishburne declared, gave the appearance that he had come "to perform a social duty and was determined to do it, so that he seldom allowed conversation to flag, although he certainly could not be said to be a great talker. He was at least a good listener."[23]

Jackson's future sister-in-law later reflected: "If, as Carlyle says, 'Genius is the capacity for infinite painstaking' . . . then Jackson possessed it; for there was no limit to the pains he would take to verify everything that came before him. Whilst he was very docile, and ready to be instructed by those whom he considered wiser than himself, it was yet curious to see how little he regarded the authority of great names. He would still persist in working out his own conclusions, and establishing facts for himself."[24]

November 22, 1851, marked a major turning point in Jackson's life. On that date he simultaneously joined the Lexington Presbyterian Church and dedicated the remainder of his life to God. The transformation into ardent Christian was instant. Col. Francis Smith, the superintendent of VMI, asserted that Jackson's new faith was "as simple as a child's in taking the word of God as his guide, and unhesitatingly accepting all therein revealed."[25]

Thereafter, as Jackson strove to be a gentleman *and* a Christian, he came more and more to see the impossibility of a man being one and not the other. He carefully marked this passage in one of his books on civility: "There should be nothing in the conduct of the Christian unpleasing to the man of the world, unless it be his godliness. His general behavior and address should be such as to offend no reasonable being, and his comity and uprightness should blunt all the arrows of hatred and envy."[26]

Jackson labored fiercely at times to overcome shyness in public. Shortly after becoming a Presbyterian, Jackson heard his pastor remark that "in our country a man who can speak [in public] multiplies himself by five." The comment made a profound impression on Jackson. He promptly joined the Franklin Literary Society of Lexington.

That was a bold step to take, for the organization contained legislators, ministers, physicians, professors—the intellectual elite of the community. One member summarized Jackson's participation: "Major Jackson undertook to enter that arena of debate, where many men of much higher pretensions were unable to hold their ground. At first it was a painful effort. It was with difficulty that he found words to express his ideas, and more than once he broke down before the end of his speech. His delivery was indistinct and his gestures ungraceful; but he persevered in the face of difficulties, for it was not in his nature to give up any thing upon which he had resolved. He spoke frequently for he was determined to learn to speak.

"His remarks were always heard respectfully for they were brief and full of strong, straight-forward common sense. By degrees he improved in his style and expression, his manner becoming more pleasing and even his gestures less awkward."[27]

Despite extreme nervousness and repeated failures, Jackson forced himself to overcome his fear of speaking in public. He took prompt advantage of his new virtue. By similarly strong effort, he became proficient at offering extemporaneous public prayer. Jackson organized a young men's Sunday school class, taught a Sunday afternoon Bible class for local slaves, helped organize the Rockbridge County Bible Society, and on one occasion gave a series of religious lectures to a crowd of strangers in his sister's hometown of Beverly.

The 1851–53 period for Jackson was a rigorous campaign of learning refinement of culture. Margaret Junkin Preston remembered his first months in Lexington. "He was of a tall, very erect figure, with a military precision about him which made us girls all account him stiff; but he was one of the most polite and courteous of men. . . . He was voted eccentric in our little professional society . . . it was only when we came to know him with the intimacy of hourly converse that we found that much that passed under the name of eccentricity was the result of the deepest underlaying principle, and compelled a respect which we dared not withhold."[28]

Jackson's friend and colleague, Raleigh Colston, agreed. "He worked hard to make up for early deficiencies. He had an improving mind and an excellent memory which retained what he read. He did not confine his efforts to reading alone but he sought to extend his knowledge by conversation upon subjects in which he felt himself deficient & which he would sometimes introduce at the most unexpected time and place."

One afternoon Colston and Jackson were walking the one hundred yards or so from the campus to downtown. Suddenly Jackson turned to him and asked: "What is poetry?" To Colston's amazement, Jackson "desired a full discussion of the subject to utilize the few minutes of our walk."[29]

Jackson's quest to become a better man accelerated. "My spare time is given to reading and to other sources of improvement," he told his sister in December 1852.[30]

His interests by then were concentrated on morality, manners, and the principal aims of life. Jackson purchased several books treating of the pursuit of civility. He placed them alongside two works he had acquired in 1848 and studied assiduously: John Bunyan's *The Pilgrim's Progress* and Lord Chesterfield's *Works of Lord Chesterfield, Including His Letters to His Son.*[31]

Bunyan's seventeenth-century allegory was one of the most popular books in the English language. Untold numbers of readers took solace from the crusade of a man named Christian who weathered the burdens of life as he sought the serenity of Paradise. Chesterfield was an eighteenth-century English lord. He had a son to whom he would pass both title and wealth. While the father was confident that the young boy would ultimately become a gentleman, he was uncertain as to how real a gentleman the youth would be. The highly cultured Chesterfield thereupon wrote hundreds of lengthy letters to the son on how to improve every aspect of his life.

Chesterfield's letters were such an international bestseller in the second quarter of the nineteenth century that they sparked a rash of books on behavior and morality. Jackson read and re-read Chesterfield. He carefully marked with pencil scores of passages he considered especially useful. One such inspiration he highlighted was the statement: "Speaking and writing, clearly, correctly, and with ease and grace, are certainly to be acquired, by reading the best authors with care, and by attention to the best living models."[32]

No single work—save the Bible—more influenced Jackson in his evolution as a polished gentleman.

Other books Jackson acquired and consulted were Joel Parker, *Invitations to True Happiness* (1844); *The Christian Keepsake and Missionary Manual for 1849* (1849), and O. S. Foster, *Memory and Intellectual Improvement Applied to Self-education and Juvenile Instruction* (1850). Jackson also derived benefit from two later works: George Winfred Hervey, *The Principles of Courtesy* (1856) and *Seventy Times Seven, or, The Law of Kindness* (1857).[33]

By 1853 Jackson had finished his basic list of maxims. The handwriting is large and meticulous, quite in contrast to Jackson's scrawling style in later years. The worn nature of the notebook gives evidence that its owner opened and closed it many times.

It was also in 1853 that Jackson received a huge boost in putting the axioms into practice. He acquired a wife. Elinor Junkin was the daughter of a Presbyterian minister and president of nearby Washington College. A year younger than Jackson, "Ellie" was physically attractive, self-assured, and possessed of a devotion to God equal to that of her husband. Most important, perhaps, it was Ellie who led Jackson away from his shell of shyness.

Jackson found in her, Margaret Preston noted, "not only the sweetest woman he had ever known, and the most charming and engaging companion, but the highest type of Christian as well. Hers was [a] . . . God-fearing faith . . . sweetened and sunned and blossom-covered by a dainty and altogether lovely womanliness. No wonder the young soldier-professor, tossed hither and thither as he had been since boyhood, found in this noble and loving woman the rest and joy of a satisfied heart; no wonder he adored her purity, reverenced her strength of conviction, and gave himself up to her guidance in spiritual matters."[34]

His new and exciting existence lasted but fourteen months. In October 1854 Ellie Jackson died in childbirth. The son she was carrying was stillborn.

For Jackson this loss was catastrophic. "She has gone on a glorious visit through a gloomy portal," he wrote his sister. To a brother-in-law, Jackson was more emotional. "I cannot realize that Ellie is gone; that my wife will no more cheer the rugged and dark way of life. The thought rushes in upon me that it is insupportable—insupportable!"[35]

Deep faith would in time overcome despair. As one means of solace, Jackson returned to a study of his book of maxims. His final entry was to personalize the collection. On the front page he wrote a dedication to Ellie. It is the concluding passage of the maxims printed here.

Thomas Jackson Arnold stated at the outset of the memoirs of his uncle: "General Jackson believed in system, method and discipline in every phase of life. He not only practiced them himself, but looked for them in others, regarding them as essential attributes towards obtaining the most out of life, utilizing the unit to produce the greatest result. He certainly regarded methodical habits as indispensable to the highest form of usefulness to others."[36]

That orderliness is easily visible in Jackson's maxims. As is shown in the accompanying commentaries, the sources for the overwhelming number of maxims are unknown. Jackson developed some from insight and experience. Others came from his extensive reading. As stated earlier, the most valuable reference work in Jackson's self-improvement was Lord Chesterfield's huge volume of letters. Jackson owned both Spanish and English editions of the book. He made extensive pencil marks in the latter, which remains part of his library. Many of Jackson's own actions and beliefs came from Lord Chesterfield's voluminous advice to his young son.

For example, at the outset the English nobleman told his heir to "look civil, as well as be so." While in Mexico, Jackson informed his sister that he had begun to dress "as a gentleman should who wishes to be received as one."[37]

One of Lord Chesterfield's first letters stated: "In order that I may not be ignorant, I read a great deal." Jackson declared that when not doing army duties, "the morning hours I occupy in studies."[38]

Lord Chesterfield implored his son to become proficient in the field of history, and he recommended as a starting point "Mr. Rollin's Ancient History." A few months after returning to the States from Mexico, Jackson wrote a friend of his newfound interest in events of the past. "I have commenced with Rollins Ancient History . . . reading from about forty to fifty pages per day."[39]

The maxims are printed here as Jackson wrote them. They are divided into the five major categories that he developed: choice of friends, rules of conversation, guides for good behavior, motives to action, and politeness and good breeding. Accompanying each maxim is a commentary that includes such material as origin of the adage, one or more quotations paralleling Jackson's statement, and the applicability of the maxim to Jackson's life. Quotations by ancient and established observers are not documented but are easily attainable in such reference works as *Bartlett's Famous Quotations* and *The Home Book of Quotations Classical and Modern*. Endnotes provide references to works that Jackson either owned or consulted frequently, as well as studies of Jackson himself.

FOLLOWING JACKSON'S death in 1863, his book of maxims disappeared. Subsequent generations could only assume that it was a casualty of time. In the late 1980s, I began work on a Jackson biography. My initial task was a nationwide search for material on the general.

One of the first depositories to respond to my queries was Tulane University. Its assistant university librarian for special collections, William E. Meneray, alerted me to a collection of papers that a Tulane alumnus and Jackson aficionado named Charles E. Davis had amassed around the turn of the twentieth century. A quick research trip to New Orleans followed. When I opened the first of three boxes of manuscripts comprising the Davis Collection, there on top of folders of papers was Jackson's book of maxims. It had lain unnoticed for eighty years.

I express lasting gratitude to Professor Meneray, and deep appreciation to Tulane University, for permission to print the book of maxims in its entirety. To the staff at the Virginia Historical Society, especially Graham T. Dozier and Gregory Stoner, I owe sincere thanks. Their assistance made it possible for me to examine at leisure the books in Jackson's library. Michael Anne Lynn and her colleagues at the Stonewall Jackson House were consistently helpful beyond the mere call of duty. Colleague William C. Davis provided his usual good encouragement. My best friend, Libba, read the manuscript with her usual thoroughness and never hesitated to point out words she did not like and phrases she did not understand. A more loving critic does not exist.

Ed Curtis and Ronald E. Pitkin of Cumberland House Publishing first suggested this volume. From start to end of the project, it was a pleasure to work with what Jackson would have called "two gentlemen."

James I. Robertson Jr.
Virginia Tech

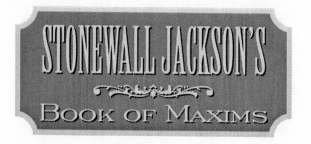

STONEWALL JACKSON'S

BOOK OF MAXIMS

SECTION I

Choice of Friends

J ACKSON WAS AWARE THAT he could achieve few goals of self-improvement without friends, but the trauma of a lonely youth made him naturally reluctant to open his heart to other people. A passage he marked in one of the books he acquired undoubtedly helped to redirect his thinking. "Childhood is a state of preparation for youth, youth for manhood, and reasoning from analogy would and does teach us that man was destined for a higher, a nobler state of existence."[1]

The more Jackson read, the more he came to see the need for friendship. Ancient philosophers pointed the way. Epicurus, in *Sovran Maxims*, proclaimed that "of all the means to insure happiness throughout the whole of life, by far the most important is the acquisition of friends." Aristotle taught in *Nichomachean Ethics*: "Without friends no one would choose to live, though he had all other goods."

Hence, Jackson took to mind the basic premise of Jacques Delille in *Malheur et Pitie* that "fate chooses our relatives, we choose our friends." Jackson carefully prepared a short list of criteria to be used in the selection of those who would be confidants. In the first half of his life, Jackson had never had more than a half-dozen real friends. Such isolation changed dramatically once he settled in Lexington. His determination, plus the love of two wives, enabled him to become a positive ingredient in society. The following were some of his guidelines.

1. A man is known by the company which he keeps.

Jackson apparently made this maxim a late addition to his list. For two-thirds of his life he had difficulty making any friends. One could hardly be discriminatory when the roster available was practically blank.

Euripides, in his *Temenidae,* was likely the first to express the thought: "Every man is like the company he is wont to keep." Variations of the adage emerged through time. Cervantes wrote: "Tell me what company thou keepest, and I'll tell thee what thou art." Jackson contemporary James Russell Lowell stated: "A man's mind is known by the company it keeps."

One of Jackson's favorite quotations from Lord Chesterfield became a constant guide: "We are, in truth, more than half what we are, by imitation. The great point is, to choose good models, and study them with care. People insensibly contract, not only the air, the manners, and the vices, of those with whom they commonly converse, but their virtues too, and even their way of thinking. . . . Persist, therefore, in keeping the best company, and you will sensibly become like them."[2]

By implication, one could conclude—as Jackson eventually did—that a person must have company to become known.

2. Be cautious in your selection.

"Young people have commonly an unguarded openness and frankness," Lord Chesterfield wrote, "they contract friendships easily. [However] if you would have your secret kept, keep it yourself; and, as it is very possible that your friend may one day or other become your enemy, take care not to put yourself in his power, while he is your friend."[3]

Secrecy became one of Jackson's strongest military weapons. He expressed logic in his explanation. "If I can keep my movements secret from my own people, I will have little difficulty in concealing them from the enemy."[4]

How to know who true friends are has always been a challenge to man. French poet Claude Mermet offered this solution: "Friends are like melons. Shall I tell you why? / To find a good one, you must a hundred try."

Like Robert E. Lee and countless other nineteenth-century American soldiers, Jackson used George Washington as a chief inspiration. Washington was "The Father of His Country," but he was also an aloof man with an elusive friendship. In 1783 Washington imparted to a young nephew wisdom that may have influenced Jackson with this maxim. "Be courteous with all but intimate with a few, and let those few be well tried before you give them your confidence. True friendship is a plant of slow growth, and must undergo and withstand the shocks of adversity before it is entitled to the appellation."[5]

3. *There is danger of catching the habits of your associates.*

Jackson agreed with Lord Chesterfield that "real friendship is a slow grower, and never thrives unless ingrained upon a stack of known and reciprocal merit."[6] Friendship required mutual cultivation, but as Jackson stated in his section on the principles of good behavior, one should learn both virtues and vices from another. A marked statement in one of Jackson's later book purchases declared: "The firm mind and the soft manner unite in forming the symmetrical character. But while we copy the wisdom of the serpent, let us never forget to displace its malevolence by the kindness of the dove."[7]

Anna Jackson observed that "discretion is the better part of valor" was a philosophy her husband often quoted. She added: "If he once lost confidence, or discovered deception and fraud on the part of one whom he had trusted, his faith was not easily restored, and he withdrew himself as much as possible from any further dealings with him. However, he religiously kept the door of his lips, not permitting a word of censure or denunciation to pass them; and even when convinced that a man was a hypocrite, his severest sentence against him was that he believed him to be a 'deceived man,' who was so blinded that he could not see the error of his ways."[8]

4. Seek those who are intelligent & virtuous & if possible those who are a little above you, especially in moral excellence.

Lord Chesterfield's influence was clearly present in the creation of this maxim. The British aristocrat told his son: "Endeavor, as much as you can, to keep company with people above you; there you rise, as much as you sink with people below you; for . . . you are whatever the company you keep is."[9]

Capt. Francis Taylor, Jackson's immediate superior in the Mexican War, was Jackson's first real counselor. It was Taylor who awakened a true religious spirit in the young lieutenant. In 1851, after Jackson had left the army, he became a member of the Lexington Presbyterian Church. Calvinist faith immediately became first his refuge, then his home, and soon his fortress.

It followed naturally that ministers would receive Jackson's attention and allegiance. They were intermediaries with the heavenly Father—superior officers in the great campaign for salvation. Jackson's reverence for such men of the cloth as his pastor, Dr. William Spottswood White in Lexington, was even more profound because Jackson always regretted lacking the talents to be a minister himself.[10]

One of his truest friends beyond clerical circles was John T. L. Preston, a prominent and wealthy Lexingtonian who had been instrumental in the establishment of the Virginia Military Institute. Preston's tender of friendship to Jackson was the embodiment of two other Chesterfield teachings: "A young man, be his merit what it will, can never raise himself; but must, like the ivy around the oak, twine himself round men of great power and prestige." Further, the surest means to acquiring character "is to observe by what particular circumstance each person pleases you the best, and imitate that person in that particular; for what pleases you will probably please another."[11]

5. It is not desirable to have a large no. of intimate friends. You may have many acquaintances but few intimate friends. If you have one who is what he should be, you are comparatively happy.

Politicians might disagree with this axiom, but mankind has generally witnessed its truth. "It is better to have one friend of great value than many friends who are good for nothing," Scythian philosopher Anacharsis concluded twenty-five hundred years ago. Benjamin Franklin gave a similar but more sweeping view of life in his 1756 edition of *Poor Richard's Almanac*: "Be civil to all; sociable to many; familiar with few; friend to one; enemy to none."

The key to why Jackson supported the idea of few close friends lies in the sentiments of English poet John Gay: "Excuse me, then! You know my heart; / But dearest friends, alas! must part."

Death and disappointment were prime ingredients in Jackson's life. The early deaths of his parents and a sister, the struggles of youth, lack of trust in people because few seemed to have trust in him—these were some of the incidents that caused Jackson to stay inside a self-created shell and not reveal his innermost thoughts. He came to feel that if one lost a mere acquaintance, the pain was minimal and short-lived. Yet if a friend departed from one's life, the emotional loss could be intense and lasting.

Jackson preferred acquaintances because he did not have too many personal feelings invested in such a relationship. From Lord Chesterfield he obtained another reason for limiting the number of friends: "Remember to make a great difference between companions and friends; for a very complaisant and agreeable companion may, and often does, prove a very improper and very dangerous friend. . . . There is a Spanish proverb which says very justly, 'Tell me who you live with, and I will tell you who you are.'"[12]

This is not to imply that Jackson was insensitive to friendships. Rather, the value he attached to them was constrained. Once during the Civil War, a colonel asked Jackson why he had appointed a highly unpopular officer to an important position. Jackson replied quickly: "As he has no friends, he will be impartial in his reports."[13]

6. That friendship may be at once fond and lasting, there must not only be equal virtue in each part, but virtue of the same kind; not only the same end must be proposed but the same means must be approved.

"Do unto others as you would have them do unto you" was a household adage in nineteenth-century America. It may have originated in one of Aristotle's thoughts: "We should behave to our friends as we would wish our friends to behave to us."

"Virtue" was a word Jackson often used. If he did not acquire it from Lord Chesterfield, the Englishman certainly reinforced its value to Jackson by declaring: "Virtue makes us pity and relieve the misfortunes of mankind; it makes us promote justice and good order in society; and, in general, contributes to whatever tends to the real good of mankind. . . . A virtuous man, under all the misfortunes of life, still finds an inward comfort and satisfaction, which makes him happier than any wicked man can be, with all the other advantages of life."[14]

In his short time as a Confederate general, the inflexible "Stonewall" judged fellow officers by two simple standards: aggressiveness in battle and faith in God. Jackson openly admired Gen. A. P. Hill and the fighting qualities he demonstrated in combat. Yet Hill was never Jackson's friend primarily because Jackson had doubts about the depths of Hill's religious feelings. In the case of Hill, the warning bell of George Winfred Hervey rang loudly in Jackson's ear: "Few friendships are lasting which are not founded on the evangelical virtue."[15]

To Jackson, friendship was a treasure that materialized slowly and embedded contentment with time. He recoiled from people who came at him eagerly or sought too strongly to be his friend. A favorite passage (marked, of course) in Lord Chesterfield stated: "Distrust all those who love you extremely upon a very slight acquaintance, and without any visible reason. Be on your guard too against those who confess, as their weaknesses, all the cardinal virtues."[16]

SECTION II

Rules of Conversation

Conversation, in its better part,
May be esteem'd a gift and not an art,
Yet much depends, as in the tiller's toil,
On culture, and the sowing of the soil.
Words learn'd by rote a parrot may rehearse,
But talking is not always to converse . . .

—William Cowper

THE ART OF CONVERSATION was the greatest hurdle Jackson had to overcome in his quest for social acceptance. He was painfully aware of seventeenth-century religious writer Thomas Fuller's warning: "He that converses not, knows nothing." Jackson also took to heart Lord Chesterfield's advice: "Every man, who can speak at all, can speak elegantly and correctly if he pleases, by attending to the best authors and orators; and, indeed, I would advise those who do not speak elegantly, not to speak at all; for I am sure they will get more by their silence than by their speech." On the other hand, the Englishman wrote: "There is hardly . . . any company, where you may not gain knowledge, if you please; almost every body knows one thing, and is glad to talk about that one thing. Seek and you will find."[1]

Conversation, Jackson soon learned, was a two-way activity. It was one thing to be able to talk intelligently about what the speaker regarded as interesting. It was also necessary to be a good listener, whether or not what you were hearing had appeal. Lord Chesterfield had guidelines for that too. "It is a great advantage for any man, to be able to talk or to hear, neither ignorantly nor absurdly, upon any subject; for I have known people, who have not said one word, hear ignorantly and absurdly; it has appeared in their inattentive and unmeaning faces. . . .

"There is nothing so brutally shocking, nor so little forgiven, as a seeming inattention to the person who is speaking to you; and I have known many a man knocked down, for (in my opinion) a much slighter provocation. . . . Nothing discovers a little, futile, frivolous mind more than this, and nothing is so offensively ill-bred."[2]

Jackson's rules of conversation reflected both sides of a verbal exchange between two people.

1. Ascertain in your conversation as well as you can wherein the skill & excellence of the individual lies & put him upon his favorite subject. Every person will of his own accord fall to talking on his favorite subject or topic if you will follow and not attempt to lead him.

Lord Chesterfield taught the axiom this way: "You will easily discover every man's prevailing vanity, by observing his favourite topic of conversation; for every man talks most of what he has most a mind to be thought to excel in. Touch him there, and you touch to the quick."[3]

George Winfred Hervey wrote a highly popular book "to illustrate and enforce the duty of Christian courtesy," and he stressed the exchange rather than what each conversationalist said. "For reconciling antipathies, overcoming prejudices, and composing differences, a blunt directness of address is not so successful as it is customary. It is a mathematical truism that the shortest distance between two points is a straight line, but courtesy would humbly advise us sometimes to unite them by a graceful curve."[4]

2. If you seek to improve in the greatest degree from the conversation of another, allow him to take his own course. If called upon, converse in turn upon your favorite topic.

The Reverend Robert L. Dabney was successively a clerical tutor and chief of staff for Jackson. The Presbyterian minister also wrote the first major biography of the general. While the narrative is often tangential and sermonic, Dabney is a good source for personal insights of his subject. He found Jackson "equally considerate of the taste and character of those with whom he held intercourse. He moulded his share of that intercourse accordingly. His scrupulous and delicate politeness made it always his aim to render others easy and comfortable in his presence."[5]

Jackson was more apt to listen than to speak. Yet he treated any conversation with a careful approach. After all, wrote Lord Chesterfield, "the characteristic of a well-bred man is, to converse with his inferiors without insolence, and with his superiors with respect and with ease." Moreover, Jackson learned, "a man who tells nothing or who talks all, will equally have nothing told him."[6]

3. *Never interrupt another but hear him out. There are certain individuals from whom little information is to be desired such as use wanton, obscene or profane language.*

No record exists of Jackson ever uttering profane or obscene words. In war, he could sometimes tolerate those who did feel the need to swear. Gens. Isaac Trimble and Richard Taylor cursed once or twice in Jackson's presence. At the battle of Cedar Mountain, a colonel shouted to his cannoneers: "Give them hell!" Jackson supposedly added: "That's right, give it to them!"[7]

The one individual who swore regularly and got away with it was Jackson's Civil War quartermaster, Maj. John A. Harman. The gruff staff officer had the reputation of being the hardest swearer in the entire Confederate army. Soldiers used to say that Harman could start a mule train a mile long by his strong language at the back end. When Jackson was within hearing distance of one of Harman's outbursts, the quartermaster escaped reproof by declaring: "There's only one language that will make mules understand!"[8]

Jackson had difficulty in not interrupting a man if he felt the speaker was being untruthful. He was incapable of escaping the definition of an "absent man." Such a person "takes no part in the general conversation; but, on the contrary, breaks into it, from time to time, with some start of his own, as if he waked from a dream. This . . . is a sure indication, either of a mind so weak that it is not able to bear above one object at a time; or so affected, that it would be supposed to be wholly engrossed by, and directed to, some very great and important subjects."[9]

4. If you speak in company, speak late.

"Silence and modesty are very valuable qualities in the art of conversation," the French philosopher Michel Montaigne taught. Jackson was a good disciple of the truism. His friend and spiritual adviser Dr. Robert Dabney commented: "He became usually an attentive but almost silent listener, and made no disclosure of his own stores of knowledge, or of profound and original reflections on the same subject; although they were often far more complete than those of the person whom he thus accepted as an instructor."[10]

Jackson made it a point to follow the advice of Horace: "The written word, unpublished, can be destroyed, but the spoken word can never be recalled."

5. *Let your words be as few as will express the sense you wish to convey & above all let what you say be true.*

This maxim is one that Jackson followed constantly. From Lord Chesterfield, he learned early: "Talk often, but never long; in that case, if you do not please, at least you are sure not to tire your hearers."[11]

Dabney attested to Jackson's brevity. "He never talked at random, even in the most unguarded moment, or on the most trivial subject. All his statements were well-considered."[12]

Jackson's sister-in-law and confidant, Margaret Junkin Preston, recalled that in group conversation Jackson often provoked smiles by his unyielding adherence to truth. "We sometimes used to charge him with losing sight of the perspective of things. Not drawing the distinction that men generally do between small and great, he laid as much stress upon the truth in the abstract . . . as in the most solemn and important."

Margaret Preston once chided "the Major" that such needless precision restricted his grace of conversation and gave an aura of stiffness. Jackson replied that he was aware of such inelegance. Nevertheless, he chose "to sacrifice all minor charms to the paramount one of absolute truth."[13]

Henry David Thoreau wrote while Jackson was compiling his maxims: "It takes two to speak the truth—one to speak, and another to hear." Another of Jackson's contemporaries, English novelist George Eliot, put the matter succinctly: "Blessed is the man who, having nothing to say, abstains from giving us wordy evidence of the fact."

6. Do not suffer your feelings to betray you into too much vehemence or earnestness or to being overbearing.

Like all men, Jackson had a temper. What set him apart from others was his ability to keep it under tight control. He participated in two years of heavy campaigning in the Civil War, yet he raised his voice fewer than a half-dozen times during the chaos. Few great historical figures have ever concealed their feelings as effectively as Jackson.

He learned from a Presbyterian publication that "if every one should obstinately persist in maintaining his own rights without considering the convenience of his fellows, nothing but contention and ill-will would ensue; but by giving way even a little, see how smoothly and pleasantly the great mass moves along. So in all relations in life we must forbear and forgive; looking not alone to our own advantage, but to the good of others."[14]

Lord Chesterfield added some appropriate words of wisdom: "Never maintain an argument with heat and clamour, though you think or know yourself to be in the right; but give your opinion modestly and coolly, which is the only way to convince."[15]

7. *Avoid triumphing over an antagonist.*

Benjamin Stillingfleet gave this poetic advice in his *Essay on Conversation:*

> Would you both please and be instructed too,
> Watch well the rage of shining to subdue.
> Hear every man upon his favourite theme,
> And ever be more knowing than you seem.

Lord Chesterfield said the same thing in prose: "There is nothing that people bear more impatiently, or forgive less, than contempt; and an injury is much sooner forgotten than an insult. If therefore you would rather please than offend, . . . remember to have that constant attention about you, which flatters every man's little vanity; and the want of which, by mortifying his pride, never fails to excite his resentment, or at least his ill will."[16]

Jackson read the Bible repeatedly. He was familiar with Proverbs 23:9: "Speak not in the ears of a fool: for he will despise the wisdom of thy words."

8. *Never engross the whole conversation to yourself.*

Undoubtedly Jackson got the idea for this maxim from Lord Chesterfield, who wrote: "Do not tell stories in company; there is nothing more tedious or disagreeable. . . . Of all things, banish the egotism out of your conversation, and never think of entertaining people with your own personal concerns, or private affairs; though they are interesting to you, they are tedious and impertinent to every body else." Later Chesterfield added: "Tell stories very seldom, and absolutely never but where they are very apt and very short."[17]

George Winfred Hervey added weight to the axiom with this observation: "We should not do for [guests] what they prefer to do for themselves, such as engrossing the conversation, instead of leading them into it, and advancing our own opinions, instead of discussing theirs."[18]

Along similar lines, philosopher Amos Alcott observed: "Time is one's best friend, teaching best of all the wisdom of silence."

"Private: T. J. Jackson," the label on the front cover of the book of maxims states. That was true in a number of respects.

Choice of friends

1. A man is known by the company which he keeps
2. Be cautious in your selection

3. There is danger of catching the habits of your associates

4. Seek those who are intelligent & virtuous & if possible those who are a little above you, especially in moral excellence

5. It is not desirable to have a large no of intimate friends you may have many acquaintances but few intimate friends If you have one who is what he should be you are comparatively happy

6. That friendship may be at once fond and lasting there must not only be equal virtue in each part, but virtue of the same kind; not only the same end must be proposed but the same means must be approved

Rules for conversation

1 Ascertain, *as in your conversation* as well as you can wherein the skill & excellence of the individual lies & put him upon his favorite subject Every person will of his own accord fall to talking on his favorite subject or topic if you will follow and not attempt to fill lead him

2 If you seek to improve in the greatest degree from the conversation of another allow him to take his own course If called upon converse in turn upon your favorite topic

3 Never interrupt another but hear him out There are certain individuals from whom little information is to be derived such as use wanton, obscene or profane language

4 If you speak in company speak late

5 Let your words be as few as will express the sense you wish to convey & above all let what you say be true

6 Do not suffer your feelings to betray you into too much vehemence, *by arguing* or to warm ostentation

7 Avoid triumphing over an antagonist

5 Never engross the whole conversation to yourself

6 ~~Speak~~ set or stand still while another is speaking to you
not dig in the earth with your feet nor take your knife from
your pocket & pare your nails nor other such actions

7 Never anticipate for another to help him out it is time
enough for you to make corrections after he has concluded if
any are necessary It is impolite to interrupt another in
his remarks

8 Say as little of yourself & friends as possible

9 Make it a rule never to accuse without due consid-
-eration any body or association of men

10 Never try to appear more wise or learned than
the rest of the company Not that you should affect
ignorance but endeavor to remain within your
own proper sphere

Let Ease & gracefulness be the standard by
which you form your estimations (taken from etiquett)

Through life let your principal object be the discharge of duty. if anything conflicts with it adhere to the former and sacrifice the latter

Be sociable — speak to all who speak to you and those whose acquaintance you do not wish to avoid hesitate not to notice them first

When in company do not endeavor to monopolize all the conversation unless such monopolization appears necessary but be content with listening and gaining information, yet converse rather than suffer conversation to draw to a close unnecessarily

2 Disregard publick opinion when it interferes with your duty

After you have formed an acquaintance with an individual never allow it to draw to a close without a cause

3 Endeavor to be at peace with all men

Never speak disrespectfully of any one without a cause

4 Endeavor to do well every thing which you undertake through preference

5 Spare no effort to suppress selfishness unless that effort would entail sorrow

6 Sacrifice your life rather than your word

Be temperate. eat too little rather than too much

7 Let your conduct towards men have some uniformity

Temperance — Eat not to dullness drink not to elevation

Silence — speak not but what may benefit others or
yourself: avoid trifling conversation

Order. Let all your things have their places: let each part
of your business have its time

8 Resolution — Resolve to perform what you ought: perform without
fail what you resolve

Frugality — Make no expense but to do good to others or
yourself i e waste nothing

Industry — Lose no time be always employed in something
usefull cut off all unnecessary actions

Sincerity — use no hurtfull deceit think innocently and justly
and if you speak ~speak~ speak accordingly

Justice — Wrong none by doing injuries or omitting the ben
efits that are your duty

Moderation — Avoid extremes: forbear resenting injuries
so much as you think they deserve

Cleanliness – Tolerate no uncleanliness in body clothes or habitation

Tranquility – Be not disturbed at trifles nor at accidents common or unavoidable

Chastity

Humility

11

"You may be what ever you resolve to be
   Motives to action (Viz)
1 Regard to your own happiness
2 Regard for the family to which you belong
3 Strive to attain a very great elevation of character
4 Fix upon a high standard of character
5 "   "   "   "   "   " action
   It is man's highest interest not to violate or attempt to
   violate the rules which which infinite wisdom has laid
   down
   The means by which men are to attain great elevation may
   be classed in three great divisions physical mental & moral
   Whatever relates to health belongs to the first
     "   "   " improvement of the mind belongs to second
   The formation of good manners & virtuous habits constitutes third

               Politeness & good-breeding
Good-breeding or politeness is the art of showing men by external
signs the internal regard we have for them. It arises from good

sense improved by good company
It must be acquired by practice and not by books

Be kind condescending & affable

Any one who has any thing to say to a fellow being to say it
with a sincere desire to please & this when ever it is done
will atone for much awkwardness in the manner of
expression

Forced complaisance is fopping & affected easiness
is ridiculous

Good breeding is opposed to selfishness vanity or pride

Endeavour to please with out lardly allowing it to be
perceived

Plain rules for attaining the character of a well bred man
1 Never weary your company by talking too long or too
frequently

2 Always look people in the face when addressing
them & generally when they address you

3 Attend to a person who is addressing you

4 Do not interrupt the person who is speaking by saying
yes or no & such like at every sentence an occasional
assent either by word or action may be well enough

Philip Dorner Stanhope (1694–1773)
The Fourth Earl of Chesterfield

He was one of the most prolific, eloquent, and perceptive writers of his age. Jackson relied heavily on Lord Chesterfield's published letters on life to his young son.

This 1851 photograph was probably taken in New York City while Jackson was stationed at Fort Hamilton. He had worn a beard in his last stages of duty in Mexico.

In 1855 Jackson sat for this photograph while visiting an aunt in Parkersburg, Virginia. The sadness of his first wife's death seems visible in his eyes.

Major Jackson of the Virginia Military Institute faculty in 1857. This rare image likely came from the Lexington studio of Samuel Pettigrew.

This lithograph (top) depicts the Virginia Military Institute as it looked in 1857 during Jackson's tenure as a professor. Faculty quarters were to the left of the main building (detail above); the laundry, hospital, and dining hall were to the right.

Elinor Junkin (1825–1854) was Jackson's first love. During the short fourteen months of their marriage, she did much to weave Jackson into Lexington society.

Anna Morrison (1831–1915) was Jackson's wife for the last six years of
his life. The "Widow of the Confederacy" never remarried.

"Ellie's" older sister, Margaret Junkin Preston (1820–1897), became Jackson's closest friend in the years immediately after the death of his first wife.

9. *Sit or stand still while another is speaking to you. [Do] not dig in the earth with your foot nor take your knife from your pocket & pare your nales nor other such action.*

This maxim seems almost silly by today's standards. That is because attentiveness today has lost much of its character. Standing solemnly at the playing of the national anthem, sitting quietly in church prior to a service, and listening to a long-winded speaker without any sign of exasperation are not distinguishable traits in present society. One of the nation's most famous television commentators has asserted that the attention-span of the average American is thirty seconds.

Jackson was disarmingly attentive. Rarely when listening to a speaker did he make any movement of restlessness. He never wavered from Lord Chesterfield's advice: "It is extremely rude not to give the proper attention, and a civil answer, when people speak to you; or to go away, or be doing something else, while they are speaking to you; for that convinces them that you despise them, and do not think it worth your while to hear or answer what they say."[19]

The only person who could not hold Jackson's attention was his pastor, Dr. William Spottswood White, in the pulpit. Jackson went to sleep at every sermon the eloquent White delivered. A noted hypnotist once visited Lexington. Townspeople packed the auditorium. When the mesmerist called for a volunteer in order to show the wonders of hypnotism, Jackson somehow came on stage. The man began his procedure; he strove hard to render Jackson unconscious. Yet Jackson continued to stare unblinkingly at the hypnotist. Finally a shout came from the audience: "No one can put Major Jackson to sleep but the Reverend Doctor White!"[20]

Jackson warned himself of scuffing the ground and of shaping fingernails while someone was talking to him. Lord Chesterfield also rebuked in conversation those people who "fix their eyes upon the ceiling or some other part of the room, look out of the window, play with a dog, twirl their snuff-box, or pick their nose."[21]

10. *Never anticipate for another to help him out. It is time enough for you to make corrections after he has concluded, if any are necessary. It is impolite to interrupt another in his remarks.*

Homer warned that "unruly manner, or ill-time applause wrong the best speaker or the justest cause."

It took Jackson a long time to conquer his tendency toward interruption when he knew (as he said in the third maxim in this category) that the speaker was wrong, or when the person talking lost Jackson in the flow of the conversation. Idle discourse was never one of Jackson's strong points because he took every word by its literal meaning.

One evening an English visitor was discussing history with Jackson. The Englishman said: "You remember, Major, that at this period Lord Burleigh was Queen Elizabeth's great counselor."

Jackson politely stopped the speaker. "No, I don't remember, for I did not know it."[22]

Any person who casually used "you know . . . you know" in conversation would constantly be interrupted by Jackson with "No, sir, I did not know. . . . No, sir, I did not know."[23]

He never used common expressions or carryovers in conversation, especially if they gave the impression of wanting to change what was. A careless remark such as "Don't you wish it would stop raining?" would bring a smile but a firm reply: "Yes, if the Maker of the weather thinks it best."[24]

11. Say as little of yourself & friends as possible.

Rousseau advised his French readers: "People who know little are usually great talkers, while men who know much say little."

Jackson was so close-mouthed that only three people (his two wives and Margaret Preston) knew the real emptiness of his first eighteen years. The social and moral collapse of his Jackson forebears left him too embarrassed to talk about antecedents. Since his friends were few in number, Jackson was left largely to speak on subjects with which he had some familiarity. That explains the long, dedicated campaign of reading that he began following the Mexican War.

Further, a deep, innate modesty blocked Jackson from speaking of himself. He learned much about the subject from Lord Chesterfield: "Above all things, and upon all occasions, avoid speaking of yourself, if it be possible. Such is the natural pride and vanity of our hearts, that it perpetually breaks out, even in people of the best parts." The Englishman added a codicil: "Cautiously avoid talking of either your own or other people's domestic affairs. Yours are nothing to them but tedious; theirs are nothing to you. The subject is a tender one: and it is odds but that you touch somebody or other's sore place."[25]

12. *Make it a rule never to accuse without due consideration any body or association of men.*

While Jackson was never dominant or accusatory in society, the same cannot be said of him as a general. He gave blind obedience to orders; he expected blind obedience from subordinates. Anything less was unacceptable. In one six-month period, Jackson placed a division commander (A. P. Hill) and two brigade commanders (Richard B. Garnett and Charles S. Winder) under arrest. A fellow officer deemed these "cruelly unjust actions" against "three of the noblest officers in our service" to be inexcusable.[26]

The general was never aware of the ancient writer Sadi's admonition: "Publish not men's secret faults, for by disgracing them you make yourself of no repute." Nor did Jackson heed the inference in Proverbs 17:9: "He that repeateth a matter separateth very friends."

13. Never try to appear more wise or learned than the rest of the company. Not that you should affect ignorance, but endeavor to remain within your own proper sphere.

Pretentiousness was not part of Jackson's makeup because his background was so empty and his faith was so full. He carried those qualities into his career as one of the world's great soldiers.

So modest was Jackson that it was not until he had lived in Lexington two years and become engaged to Elinor Junkin that her family learned of his distinguished record in the Mexican War.[27]

Natural diffidence blocked Jackson from vanity. Lord Chesterfield was outspoken but correct in the value of modesty. It "engages and captivates the minds of people; as, on the other hand nothing is more shocking and disgustful than presumption and impudence. We cannot like a man who is always commending and speaking well of himself, and who is the hero of his own story; on the contrary, a man who endeavours to conceal his own merit, who sets that of other people in its true light, who speaks but little of himself, and with modesty: such a man makes a favourable impression upon the understanding of his hearers, and acquires their love and esteem."[28]

14. Let ease & gracefulness be the standard by which you form your estimation (taken from etiquett).

Dr. William Spottswood White, Jackson's pastor in Lexington, watched with interest as Jackson waged his campaign to become more socially acceptable. White penned an interesting summary. "Genl. Jackson was a man whom it was no easy matter to know . . . because there was a breadth and depth of character about him that would never be suspected by the superficial and the bigoted. He was preeminently considerate of the taste and character of those with whom he held intercourse and carefully shaped his intercourse accordingly. He was one of the most scrupulously and delicately polite men I ever knew, and hence it was always his aim to make others easy & comfortable in his presence.

"His first thought on meeting with others seemed to be what objects of conversation will be most familiar to their thoughts and most consonant with their feelings. He never introduced a subject merely because it was one with which he was most familiar or on which he could make a display of himself. With a preacher or a lady he never introduced party politicks or the best method of making or repelling an attack in battle. Hence, one might be on terms of great intimacy with him for months or even years, and yet know nothing of him whatever as a scientific or military man. In this trait of character must be sought a solution of the fact that he was so great a man & yet so little known."[29]

Jackson learned well that "the cheerful Christian seems always at peace with himself, and with all the world. A gentle animation is constantly welling up in his soul, and diffusing its cheerful influence over all his faculties."[30]

SECTION III

Guides for Good Behavior

THIS IS THE LONGEST section in Jackson's maxims, in part because it is the most encompassing, and in part because Jackson considered them the most important of the guidelines. Here earthly and spiritual topics began blending. Such leads naturally to the ambition of Thomas Jackson.

His army physician, Dr. Hunter McGuire, commented: "Under the grave and generally serious manner, sometimes almost stern, there were strong human passions, dominated by his iron will—there was earthly ambition. . . . There was in this great soldier a deep love for all that is true, for the beautiful, for the poetry of life, and a wealth of rich and quick imagination for which few would give him credit. Ambition! Yes, far beyond what ordinary men possess. And yet, he told me when talking in my tent one dreary night . . . that he would not exchange one moment of his life hereafter, for all the earthly glory he could win."[1]

On the other hand, McGuire testified to Jackson's "natural appetites for glory, until corrected by grace."[2] His basic rule was to attain advancement whenever possible but never unless it was merited. Jackson drew a fine line between fame and notoriety. That is one of the keys to understanding the man.

Ambition was never a virtue in his eyes. Seeking earthly gain conflicted with faith in God and invited divine punishment. In one of his books Jackson double-marked this passage: "It should be our purpose to perform, not great actions, but just, kind, meek, and self-denying actions. . . . The moment we lose sight of the disparity between Infinite Protection and our own moral character, we are in danger of exalting ourselves in the sight of our fellow-men."[3]

In the last decade of Jackson's life, his pilgrimage became to walk humbly even while winning acclaim. Doing so would be consistent with his faith. His advancements would be to God's glory rather than man's glorification.

1. *Through life let your principal object be the discharge of duty; if anything conflicts with it, adhere to the former and sacrifice the latter.*

According to his wife, Jackson often said: "My duty is to obey orders!"[4] This dedication became deep-rooted during Jackson's ten years as a professor at VMI. One of the Institute's trustees considered "the striking characteristic" of Jackson to be "his strict sense of duty. This with an abrupt manner and a crisp but not brusque form of expression did not tend to render him popular."[5]

The Reverend R. L. Dabney asserted that duty was "the ever present and supreme sentiment" in Jackson's makeup. Another clerical friend, Dr. Moses Hoge, wrote a month after Jackson's death: "If he required implicit obedience to his orders, he set the example of prompt and unhesitating compliance with those he received himself."[6]

General Jackson was never absent from his post of duty. Not once did he take a furlough or brief leave to visit a loved one or attend to a personal errand. Duty came first. Late in 1862, one of his aides lamented that he had not been away from the army for a day since he entered service.

"Very good," Jackson replied. "I hope you will be able to say so after the war is over."[7]

Be sociable—speak to all who speak to you and those whose acquaintance you do not wish to avoid, hesitate not to notice them first.

German philosopher Arthur Schopenhauer observed: "Politeness is to human nature what warmth is to wax." Jackson contemporary Ralph Waldo Emerson likewise noted: "Life is short, but there is always time for courtesy."

George Winfred Hervey, a major source for Jackson's efforts at self-improvement, wrote in a passage that Jackson marked: "The hearts of the worldly are not affected by heroic acts of self-denial, but they are captivated by the refined attentions of Christian kindness. . . . Courtesy claims the dignity of a Christian virtue, originating in divine grace, and constantly dependent on it for vigor and growth. . . . It prompts the man of the world to show respect for a superior, esteem for an equal, or kindness to an inferior. . . . The social feelings express themselves by a language generally tender, sometimes elegant."[8]

Rudeness was never present in Jackson's personality. Throughout his life he adhered to Lord Chesterfield's precept: "It is not sufficient to deserve well, one must please well too. Awkward, disagreeable merit will never carry anybody far."[9]

When in company, do not endeavor to monopolize all the conversation unless such monopolization appears necessary, but be content with listning and gaining information, yet converse rather than suffer conversation to draw to a close unnecessarily.

This is a repetition of at least five of Jackson's earlier maxims treating directly or indirectly of listening. The emphasis here seems to have been on allowing conversation to end naturally and pleasantly. Emerson once observed: "Talking is like playing the harp; there is as much laying the hands on the strings to stop their vibration as in twanging them to bring out their music."

Jackson became reasonably successful at ending a conversation—with one glaring exception. Having little sense of humor, he never understood jokes. Maj. Raleigh Colston spoke for the VMI faculty and student body by commenting: "It was a settled opinion with us that Jackson could never see a joke and was utterly incapable of appreciating a pun."[10]

A quarter-century after the Civil War, Hunter McGuire recalled of the general: "He was a difficult man to joke with, and it was not a safe thing always to try it. . . . I used to tell him some little jokes that were going on in the army, but they had to be very plain ones for him to see them."

On those rare occasions when Jackson did laugh, McGuire continued, "he did it with his whole heart. He would catch one knee with both hands, lift it up, throw his body back, open wide his mouth, and his whole face and form be convulsed with mirth—but there was no sound."[11]

Perhaps Jackson never learned how to laugh; or possibly he adhered firmly to Lord Chesterfield's doctrine: "Frequent and loud laughter is the characteristic of folly and ill manners; it is the manner in which the mob express their silly joy at silly things; and they call it being merry. In my mind, there is nothing so illiberal, and so ill bred, as audible laughter."[12]

2. *Disregard public opinion when it interfears with your duty.*

The most famous American contemporary of Jackson's age had strong views on public opinion. In speeches given in the 1859–60 period, Abraham Lincoln proclaimed: "Public opinion in this country is everything. . . . Public opinion settles every question here—any policy to be permanent must have public opinion at the bottom."[13]

Two English writers of the time disagreed. Alfred Austin dismissed public opinion as "no more than what people think that other people think," while William C. Hazlitt asserted: "Nothing is more unjust or capricious than public opinion."

President Ulysses S. Grant watched corruption defile his cabinet. "No personal consideration should stand in the way of performing a public duty," Grant declared.[14] On that point, Jackson and Grant were in agreement.

Once during the war, Jackson defined "the right sort of man" to an aide. Such an individual was "one always striving to do his duty and never satisfied if anything can be done better."[15]

He never wavered from his belief that all human feelings were subservient to those pertaining to duty—especially when earthly chores and the work of the Lord were one and the same. A West Point friend and fellow Confederate general became less impressed with Jackson as the Civil War unfurled. "He was always very firm," Gen. Chase Whiting complained, "and in the military part of his life had no compromise in him."[16]

After you have formed an acquaintance with an individual, never allow it to draw to a close without a cause.

Friends are always more easily made than kept. The great test of friendship is time. Samuel Johnson warned that friendships can be "like plants that bear their fruit and die."

Hence the English lexicographer urged every man to "keep his friendship in constant repair." Or, as Benjamin Franklin expressed it in *Poor Richard's Almanac,* "be slow in choosing a friend, slower in changing."

Undoubtedly, some of Jackson's friendships became strained because of his meticulousness and rigid set of values. (In the 1850s Jackson was always somewhat of a problem for Col. Francis H. Smith, the VMI superintendent who hired him.) The fact that his real friends were so few kept Jackson conscious of the need not to let such amity lapse unnecessarily. The Athenian scholar Solon offered a principle that Jackson could accept: "Do not be rash to make friends, and when once they are made, do not drop them."

3. *Endeavor to be at peace with all men.*

In *The Song of Hiawatha*, Henry Wadsworth Longfellow urged: "Therefore be at peace henceforward and as brothers live together." This Jackson found impossible to do fully. A sister-in-law and very close observer wrote of Jackson: "We never succeeded in winning him to the avowal of adverse judgment, unless there were overt acts which were patent to everybody. Then his denunciation went beyond those of other persons. If a man once deceived him, he never afterwards gave him credit for any truthfulness."[17]

Jackson marked this passage in one of his favorite books: "Evil-speaking is the sin which, in social life, requires our most constant watchfulness. Let us pray each morning not to be led into this temptation, but that we may have our hearts filled with charity which suffereth long and is kind, which believeth no evil, and giveth tongue to no slanderous report."[18]

The general's mapmaker, Maj. Jed Hotchkiss, stated after the Civil War: "He was uncompromising and exacting in requiring obedience to orders, always obeying them strictly himself, and was swift to punish willful disobedience or careless neglect, but I never heard him use a word of disparagement of any one, not even of those who spoke and wrote falsely and evilly of himself."[19]

Never speak disrespectfully of any one without a cause.

Anna Jackson was proud of her husband's calm demeanor. "He was utterly free from censoriousness, envy, detraction, and all uncharitableness, and certainly kept his rule that if he could not say something good of a man, he would not speak of him at all."[20]

Jackson's nephew echoed those sentiments: "His bearing and demeanor were invariably that of a thoughtful and polite gentleman. One never heard General Jackson express unfavorable criticism of others. Yet his judgment of men was very apt to be correct; this was observable by his avoiding as far as possible having anything to do with those of whose methods he disapproved. He did nothing by word or act to injure them; he let them alone."

If Jackson doubted the honesty of a merchant, he stopped doing business at that store.[21]

4. *Endeavor to do well evry thing which you undertake through prefrence.*

When Jackson was twenty years old and a West Point cadet, he wrote his sister: "Be not discouraged by disappointments and difficulties, but on the contrary let each stimulate you to greater exertions for attaining noble ends, and an approving conscience at least will be your reward."[22]

Henry David Thoreau lent credence to that precept with the statement: "I know of no more encouraging fact than the unquestionable ability of man to elevate his life by a conscious endeavor."

A word never associated with Jackson was slothfulness. He put heart and soul into everything he attempted. If he was ever aware of "a second chance" at something, he never mentioned it. The effort, whatever it might be, had to be concentrated. "Awkwardness," Lord Chesterfield wrote, "is a more real disadvantage than it is generally thought to be; it often occasions ridicule, it always lessens dignity."[23]

Of course, in the matter of faith, Jackson's endeavors never waned. A minister friend stated: "To the glory of a soldier always invincible in battle, he added the high moral glory of a Christian always faithful to the Lord. While eminent for many things, he was pre-eminent for his abiding trust in God. . . . He was a man of God first and last, and always."[24]

5. Spare no effort to suppress selfishness unless that effort would entail sorrow.

Ovid remarked two thousand years ago that "everyone was eloquent in behalf of his own cause." Frenchman Michel Montaigne later emphasized: "He that lives not somewhat to others, liveth little to himself."

Christian humility and human selfishness cannot coexist in a person. Jackson demonstrated such a truism following the 1861 battle of First Manassas. Although he had been clearly the premier hero in the Confederate victory, public accolades were going to other commanders. Anna Jackson complained of the oversights to her husband. Jackson replied that his superiors understandably would and should get the praise. "I am thankful to an ever kind Heavenly Father that he makes me content to await His own good & pleasure for commendation, knowing that 'all things work together for any good.'"[25]

Benjamin Franklin warned in *Poor Richard's Almanac*: "He that falls in love with himself, will have no rivals." Jackson never exhibited selfishness; he surely regarded it as one of the great curses of mankind because of its conflict with faith in God.

6. Sacrifice your life rather than your word.

An English writer wrote shortly after Jackson's death: "The perseverance he displayed in his studies [at West Point] grew in time into the determined, indomitable courage, that was conspicuous throughout his subsequent career. It was a perseverance that might have grown into stubbornness, had it not been combined with benevolence and other Christian graces."[26]

Lord Chesterfield similarly had much to say about truth and keeping one's word. "Nothing is more essential than always to speak truth, and to be strictly observant of [its] promise. On the other hand, nothing is more infamous and dishonourable than to tell lies and break our word."

In a subsequent letter, Chesterfield observed: "Breaking of your word is a folly, a dishonour, and a crime. It is a folly, because nobody will trust you afterwards; and is both a dishonour and a crime, truth being the first duty of religion and morality; and whoever has not truth, cannot be supposed to have any one good quality, and must become the detestation of God and man."[27]

Be temperate—eat too little rather than too much.

Jackson had no difficulty in following this tenet, for his eating habits were strange if not erratic. He was a long-time sufferer of dyspepsia. This nineteenth-century term was a catchall word for any form of impaired digestion.

Therefore, Margaret Preston noted, Jackson "ate, as he did everything else, from a sense of duty."[28] He "professed *absolute* control of appetite for food. . . . Went to work in a business-like way to study hygiene & digestion, and was quite learned therein."[29]

An aide, Lt. Kyd Douglas, witnessed Jackson's eating habits during the war and concluded: "He liked a great many things he did not eat, and ate some things he did not like. He was not a hearty eater, although at times he had a good appetite. Whatever might be the variety before him he generally selected one or two things only for his meal. . . . He was, therefore, at times a great disappointment to hospitable housewives, who, after skillfully providing various handiworks of choice food for his enjoyment, looked on regretfully when he selected one or two simple things and declined all the rest."[30]

Jackson never used pepper. He claimed that doing so paralyzed his right leg.[31]

7. *Let your conduct towards men have some uniformity.*

John D. Imboden was a prewar acquaintance and served under Jackson for extended periods during the Civil War. Imboden remembered: "He was the easiest man in our army to get along with pleasantly so long as one did his duty . . . he would over-look serious faults if he saw they were the result of ignorance, and would instruct the offender in a kindly way. He was as cour-teous to the humblest private who sought an interview for any purpose as to the highest officer in his command. He despised superciliousness and self-assertion, and nothing angered him so quickly as to see an officer wound the feelings of those under him by irony and sarcasm."[32]

One of Jackson's favorite ministers, Dr. Moses D. Hoge, like-wise recalled: "Unlike some military men, who seem to delight in making subordinate officers feel their disparity of rank, he never seemed to think of rank at all, and was as polite to a pri-vate as to the President. In riding through his camp, when the men saluted him as he passed, he invariably raised his cap from his head, instead of returning the abrupt recognition of their courtesy with which some officers content themselves."[33]

There was a condition or two attached to Jackson's behavior. Capt. William W. Blackford, a cavalry staff officer, observed: "Stonewall Jackson was very pleasant and agreeable when he chose to be so and when his mind was at ease, but he was not the man to talk to when he was busy, by any manner of means."[34]

Temperance—Eat not to dullness, drink not to elevation.

If Jackson's eating habits were austere, his use of liquor was all but nonexistent. Only three times in his Confederate career did Jackson drink an intoxicant. On each occasion, it was for medicinal purposes.

The reason Jackson avoided alcohol so fanatically was that he liked the taste. According to an aide, Jackson once observed: "I can sip whiskey or brandy with a spoon with the same pleasure the most delicious coffee or cordial would give you. I am the fondest man of liquor in this army and if I had indulged my appetite, I would have been a drunkard. But liquors are not good for me. I question whether they are much good to anyone."[35]

Jackson remained insistent to the end that, for good health, people should eat what they do not like.

Silence—speak not but what may benefit others or yourself; avoid trifling conversation.

Since Jackson avidly read the Bible, he would have been familiar with the statement in Proverbs: "Even a fool, when he holdeth his peace, is counted wise." English essayist William C. Hazlitt later modified the thought: "Silence is one great art of conversation. He is not a fool who knows when to hold his tongue."

As a commander in the field, Jackson combined silence with secrecy. A lieutenant in the first weeks of the Civil War wrote home: "Ma, we dont know one hour where we may be the next. Col. Jackson never lets anyone know his intentions."[36]

Such silence became infectious with his troops. Jackson once accosted a straggler and asked the man to what unit he was attached. "I don't know," came the reply. Jackson continued questioning the soldier. The same answer was all that he got. Finally, an angry Jackson snapped: "What do you know, sir?"

The private replied promptly: "I know that old Stonewall ordered us not to know anything, and damned if I ain't going to stick to it!"[37]

Order—Let all your things have their places: let each part of your business have its time.

If Jackson had ever marked his Bible, he would have highlighted the passage in Ecclesiastes that begins: "To every thing there is a season, and a time to every purpose under the heaven: a time to be born, and a time to die; a time to plant and a time to pluck up that which is planted."

Perfect system and regularity marked Jackson's home life and military itineraries. In Lexington, one could almost set a watch by the preciseness of Jackson's daily routine. His Confederate schedule was more encumbered and unpredictable, but organization prevailed whenever possible to promote orderliness.

Punctuality, wrote Margaret Preston, "was one of Jackson's most marked characteristics; no one could ever charge him with loss of time through dilatoriness on his part. He never failed to fill an engagement. . . . He was rigid as to the hours of his meals, and when I would remind him, if dinner was five minutes late, that cooks were human, he was accustomed to say, 'I don't mind the five minutes delay beyond time, but I do beg that you will not let me know of it.'"[38]

Although a master of military surprises, Jackson did not like surprises in his own life. He obeyed Lord Chesterfield's advice: "Have order and method in your accounts, in your reading, in the allotment of your time; in short, in every thing. You cannot conceive how much time you will save by it, nor how much better every thing you do will be done."[39]

8. *Resolution—Resolve to perform what you aught: perform without fail what you resolve.*

Here Jackson equated resolution with promptness and determination. Another of Lord Chesterfield's teachings was a commandment for Jackson: "Never procrastinate, never put off till to-morrow what you can do to-day; and never do two things at one time: pursue your object, be what it will, steadily and indefatigably; and let any difficulties (if surmountable) rather animate than slacken your endeavours. Perseverance has surprising effects."[40]

Once Jackson's mind was set, no deviation broke the resolve. Sister-in-law Margaret Preston declared: "He had less regard for mere authority than any man I ever knew; and though never troubled by speculative doubts, we used to tell him that he had too daring a confidence in the infallibility of his own convictions."[41]

English poet Abraham Cowley might have had Jackson in mind (had Cowley not been writing two centuries earlier) when he wrote: "His way once chose, he forward thrust outright, / Nor stepped aside for dangers or delight." Jackson himself embraced the teachings of George Winfred Hervey: "The ability to encounter danger and difficulties with fearlessness and composure, is a quality as serviceable as it is ornamental to every true knight of the cross."[42]

Frugality—Make no expinse but to do good to others or yourself: i.e., waste nothing.

Born in poverty, raised with few personal means, Jackson never adopted in any area the habits of a spendthrift. Every purchase was the result of careful thought; every investment came after prolonged consideration. The words of Samuel Johnson applied well to Jackson: "Without frugality none can be rich, and with it very few would be poor."

If Jackson had anything akin to what today might be regarded an extravagance, it was his annual habit of tithing to his church.

Lord Chesterfield was again Jackson's beacon in this self-improvement: "A fool squanders away, without credit or advantage to himself, more than a man of sense spends with both. . . . The former buys whatever he does not want, and does not pay for what he does want. . . . Keep an account, in a book, of all that you receive, and of all that you pay; for no man, who knows what he receives and what he pays, ever runs out."[43]

Industry—Lose no time; be always employed in something usefull; cut off all unnecessary actions.

Jackson was so regimented as a college professor, so energetic as a field commander, that it is difficult to imagine him not constantly occupied in some endeavor. In his copy of an early Andrew Jackson biography, the Major highlighted this passage: "Promptitude and decision, and activity in execution, constituted the leading traits of Jackson's character."[44]

Benjamin Franklin was a more precise guide. "When men are employed, they are best contented; for on the days they worked they were good-natured and cheerful, and, with the consciousness of having done a good day's work, they spent the evening jollily; but on our idle days they were mutinous and quarrelsome."

Naturally, Lord Chesterfield instructed his son repeatedly on the advantages of industry over sloth. "A man of sense knows how to make the most of time, and puts his whole sum either to interest or to pleasure: he is never idle, but constantly employed either in amusements or in study. It is a saying, that idleness is the mother of all vice."[45]

Sincerity—Use no hurtfull deceit: think innocently and justly, and if you speak, speak accordingly.

A passage from Psalms 101 would have been enough inspiration for Jackson here: "He that worketh deceit shall not dwell within my house: he that telleth lies shall not tarry in my sight."

George Winfred Hervey taught Jackson a series of principles on sincerity. "A behavior marked by simplicity always becomes the child of God. . . . Innocence needs no covering. . . . Manners can never be separated from morals. . . . Ill-timed and ill-placed actions are seldom repulsive when they are recommended by honesty and frankness."[46]

Emerson believed that "never was a sincere word utterly lost." More than one philosopher has averred that sincerity is more valuable than knowledge. The truth of such a belief is obvious: what a person feels instinctively has more to do with his being than the mere acquisition of facts. Knowing "how" is more beneficial than knowing "what."

Justice—Wrong none by doing injuries or omitting the benefits that are your duty.

For Jackson, this axiom was easily said, all but impossible to implement as a soldier. Plato once observed: "To do injustice is more disgraceful than to suffer it." Not so with Jackson who, in the matter of justice, was truly "Stonewall."

The Thomas Jackson who was a soldier in the Civil War was fighting not so much for country as for God. (One needed faith before patriotism.) For Jackson, the struggle between North and South was a conflict seeking God's redemption for unknown sins. That side that displayed the deeper and more abiding faith would assuredly triumph. Therefore, the highly pious Jackson entered the war with the attitude of one embarking on a religious crusade. He would tolerate no earthly interference. A soldier who failed to obey a Jackson order was guilty of two crimes: disobedience and heresy.

Two Civil War staff officers voiced parallel opinions of Jackson in the matter of justice. Lt. Kyd Douglas wrote: "General Jackson was as hard as nails; in the performance of a duty he always was. . . . [Although] a gentleman of tender impulses and kind heart, he seemed to have a horror of cruelty. Why was this? Simply because in duty he was governed by his judgment alone, by a strict construction of his sense of justice, by the demands of the public service. There was no place for sentiment or pity. In the execution of the law he was inexorable, justice and mercy seemed out of place."[47]

Chief of staff Robert L. Dabney commented: "To his Colonels he was a stricter master than to his private soldiers; and to his Generals, more exacting than to his Colonels. If he found in an officer a hearty and zealous purpose to do all his duty, with a willing and self-sacrificing courage and devotion, he was, to him, the most tolerant and gracious of superiors. . . . But, if he believed that his subordinates were self-indulgent or contumacious, he became a stern and exacting master, seeming ever to watch for an opportunity to visit their shortcomings upon them."[48]

Moderation—Avoid extremes: forbear resenting injuries so much as you think they deserve.

A fundamental of life, Lord Chesterfield advised, "is the mastery of one's temper, and the coolness of mind, and serenity of countenance, which hinders us from discovering, by words, actions, or even looks, those passions or sentiments by which we are inwardly moved or agitated. . . .

"Make yourself absolute master of your temper and your countenance, so far, at least, as that no visible change does appear in either, whatever you may feel inwardly. This may be difficult, but it is by no means impossible; and, as a man of sense never attempts impossibilities on one hand, on the other, he is never discouraged by difficulties."[49]

Jackson always sought to follow Lord Chesterfield's principles. In this case, however, he would have leaned more to Thomas Paine's caveat: "A thing moderately good is not so good as it ought to be. Moderation in temper is always a virtue, but moderation in principle is always a vice."

Cleanliness—Tolerate no uncleanliness in body, clothes or habitation.

After he found a religious home in 1851, Jackson associated everything in life with his faith. John Wesley's great beatitude, "cleanliness, indeed, is next to godliness," had Jackson's support. So did Francis Bacon's belief that "cleanness of the body was ever deemed to proceed from a due reverence to God."

Anna Jackson wrote that her husband's dress "was always in good taste and faultlessly neat. Everything he wore was of the best material."[50] A nephew added: "In the care of his person and dress he was unusually neat and tidy. I never knew any one to be more particular in this respect than he was."[51]

Tranquility—Be not disturbed at trifles nor at accidents common or unavoidable.

Alexander Pope put Jackson's feelings into a couplet: "At ev'ry trifle scorn to take offence; / That always shows great pride or little sense."

Jackson accepted life for the bumpy journey it was. He would not let human distractions block him from his chosen route. Tranquility, patience, and calmness were Jackson trademarks. Surgeon Hunter McGuire said of him: "The imperturbable coolness of a great commander was pre-eminently his. He was always calm and self-controlled."[52]

That was not completely true. Maj. Robert L. Dabney recalled three occasions when Jackson's "fiery spirit fairly broke from his customary restraints." They were climactic moments in the battles of Winchester, Gaines' Mill, and Cedar Mountain.[53]

A famous example of Jackson's tranquility (or perhaps merely custom) concerned his habit of saying "very commendable" as a standard reply to messages. During a summer 1862 engagement, Jackson turned from the battle to ask an aide why a certain courier had not returned from delivering one of his dispatches. The aide replied that the messenger had been killed. "Very commendable," said Jackson as he turned back to the action.[54]

Chastity

This is the most perplexing of all of Jackson's maxims. He himself was twenty-nine years old when he fell in love for the first time. He was never known for an affair, illicit or otherwise.

Following the death of his first wife, Jackson and sister-in-law Margaret Junkin gravitated in their grief toward one another. Indications are strong that love soon blossomed. By the tenets of the Presbyterian Church at that time, however, Thomas and Margaret were not in-laws; they were brother and sister. They could never wed. Jackson thereupon began searching for a new wife. Margaret soon married a long-time Lexington acquaintance. Fortunately, friendship filled the gap where once romance was embedded.

Of course, Jackson was strait-laced where morals were concerned. A Presbyterian clergyman married a divorced lady. Jackson voiced no opinion; however, whenever the minister was conducting services in Lexington, Jackson would not attend.

Secondary definitions of "chastity" include decency and simplicity of style. Jackson was a disciple of those behavioral patterns as well.

Humility

Surely Jackson was familiar with Proverbs 16: "The fear of the Lord is the instruction of wisdom; and before honour is humility."

Anna Jackson commented that Jackson's humility "was as pre-eminent as his conscientiousness."[55] Biographer and friend Robert L. Dabney asserted: "Unaffected modesty was imprinted upon his countenance, and every trait of his manners. No man ever lived who was further removed from egotism."[56]

One of Jackson's "good conduct" books contains these double-marked passages: "Humility is but charity bowing to do homage and stooping to deeds of kindness. . . . It endeavors to sink beneath the notice of the world, and yet its very self-abasement excites the wonder and wins the praise of all. . . . The man that humbles himself before his enemy while is yet smarting under wrong and abuse, shows a spirit superior to the flesh . . . and a wisdom that prefers peace to his own rights."[57]

A brother-in-law and comrade in arms, Confederate Gen. D. Harvey Hill, wrote after the Civil War: "Jackson was truly a modest man. He would blush like a school-girl at a compliment. He was easily confused in the presence of strangers, especially if they were ladies. It is well known that the noisy demonstrations which the troops always made when they saw him were painfully embarrassing to him. This was usually attributed to his innate modesty; but that was not the sole cause. . . . In the last interview I ever had with him, he said: 'The manner in which the press, the army, and the people seem to lean upon certain persons is positively frightful. They are forgetting God in the instruments He has chosen. It fills me with alarm.'"[58]

"You may be what ever you will resolve to be."

Jackson put this most famous of his maxims in quotation marks for at least two reasons. One was that he extracted the statement from a little-known source. A decade ago, Prof. Charles Royster revealed that the quotation first appeared in a work by Joel Hawes, a Connecticut minister.[59] Hawes stated in *Lectures to Young Men, on the Formation of Character* (1851, p. 74): "My friends, *you may be whatever you resolve to be. Resolution is omnipotent.* Determine that you will be something in the world, and you shall be something. Aim at excellence, and excellence will be attained. This is the great secret of effort and eminence."

The second reason Jackson placed the statement in quotation marks stemmed from years of using the thought before he saw it in print. While home on furlough from West Point in 1844, Jackson reportedly told a cousin: "I am going to make a man of myself if I live. What I will to do I can."[60]

According to his wife, Jackson often declared: "One can always do what he wills to accomplish."[61]

Near the outbreak of civil war, a friend asked Jackson if he had been unsure of himself when he left the army for the totally unfamiliar life of a college professor. Jackson replied: "No, I expected to be able to study sufficiently in advance of my class, for one can always do what he willed to accomplish."[62]

SECTION IV

Motives to Action

HERE JACKSON APPEARED TO step back and peer at life in its broadest view. What he outlined was the framework for his efforts. Inside it he placed the larger goals he sought in life's journey.

Some of the statements in this category may seem unaffected and a bit repetitious. If so, it's because Jackson stated the thoughts a second time for emphasis. It also must be remembered that whether in civilian or in military life, he devoted assiduous attention to duties likely to win him public respect.

The pains to which he went ultimately formed the man he wanted to be. The Reverend James R. Graham came to know Jackson well, for the general lived with the Winchester minister for several months in the 1861–62 period. Graham later summarized Jackson by writing: "His manners, it is true, would not be pronounced 'courtly,' but neither were they constrained. In his bearing there was nothing of stateliness, but neither was there of awkward embarrassment. His figure was not ungainly, nor his movement uncouth. He was no Chesterfield—no paragon, whose air and presence compelled the admiration of all beholders. He was just a simple gentleman."[1]

1. Regard to your happiness.

George Sand once noted that "there is only one happiness in life, to love and be loved." The absence of familial love throughout most of Jackson's childhood was a crippling void that created an adult personality shy, quiet, withdrawn, humorless, and generally lacking in the basic joys of life. Jackson craved to give and to receive love. Not until far past the midway point of his brief life did he become familiar with the uplifting emotions of romantic love.

A century before Jackson, William Cowper wrote: "Thus happiness depends, as Nature shows, / Less on exterior things than most suppose." Prior to Jackson's two marriages, he found the seeds for happiness in one of the first books he purchased. The author gave these encouragements:

"All men seek happiness. The gay dance of pleasure, the toils of business, the pursuits of learning, and the struggles of ambition, alike take their rise in the desire of enjoyment. No human being can be found on earth so wretched as not to indulge the hope of good. . . . Has God created us with such a desire without providing the means of its gratification?" . . . God constituted you for happiness, and that happiness is to be achieved only by deliberately choosing the service of the Lord as the great end of living."[2]

2. *Regard for the family to which you belong.*

In the early nineteenth century, the Jackson family held a prominent place in the politics and society of northwestern Virginia. Yet the family's prestige collapsed with the generation of Thomas Jackson's father. The son often declared that he longed to restore the prominence of the Jackson name. In a letter to his sister about the VMI faculty post he hoped to secure, Jackson said: "I consider the position both conspicuous and desirable." A few lines later, he added: "I have some hopes that our ancient reputation may be revived."[3]

The adult Jackson yearned for the things he had never had as an impressionable youth: a real home, a family atmosphere, the collective love that such an association fosters. With marriage in 1853 to Elinor Junkin, he became happier than he had ever been. Ellie's sudden death fourteen months later all but shattered Jackson's spirit.

In July 1857 he married Mary Anna Morrison. "I hope in the course of time we shall be able to call some house our home," he told a friend. "I have taken the first important step by securing a wife capable of making a happy home, and the next thing is to give her an opportunity."[4]

A daughter born to the Jacksons lived only a few days. This time he could accept death as God's will and continue to seek happiness. He found it in the atmosphere of home life. Anna Jackson remembered: "He believed in providing his family with every comfort and convenience, for which he spared no expense."[5]

Margaret Preston provided a greater insight. "Only in the innermost circle of home did any one come to know what Jackson was really like. His natural temperament was extremely buoyant, and his cheerfulness and *abandon* were beautiful to see, provided there were only one or two people to see it. He was exceedingly fond of children, and would roll with them over the carpet, play them all manner of tricks, and amuse them endlessly with his Spanish baby-talk."[6]

Jackson would have agreed with educator Charles W. Eliot's assertion that "the security and elevation of the family and of family life are the prime objects of civilization, and the ultimate end of all industries."

3. *Strive to attain a very great elevation of character.*

"Character is higher than intellect," Ralph Waldo Emerson taught. Lord Chesterfield cautioned his son that character "is the sure and solid foundation upon which you must both stand and rise. A man's moral character is a more delicate thing than a woman's reputation for chastity. A slip or two may possibly be forgiven her . . . but a man's moral character once tainted is irreparably destroyed."[7]

Jackson's success in character building approached perfection. An early biographer concluded: "Jackson's personal character was absolutely without blemish. His habits were of the manliest that a Puritan could wish; his honor clean, and his courage superlative; while as a gentleman in expression and action, he had no superior."[8]

A man who would not use liquor, tobacco, or profanity, Jackson could be a role model for any age.

4. Fix upon a high standard of character.

For Jackson, it was one thing to gain high character and another to maintain it. While evangelist Dwight L. Moody liked to say that character "is what you are in the dark," Abraham Lincoln used a metaphor: "Character is like a tree and reputation like its shadow. The shadow is what we think of it; the tree is the real thing."

One of Jackson's military aides made this analysis of the general's deportment. "In manner he was deferential, modest, and retiring, in the presence of women diffident to excess. He never blustered and even on the field of battle was rarely severe except to incompetency and neglect. He judged himself more harshly than anyone else did, but towards the weakness of others he had abundant charity."[9]

Jackson was ever aware of Lord Chesterfield's perception: "There is nothing so delicate as your moral character, and nothing which it is in your interest so much to preserve pure. Should you be suspected of injustice, malignity, perfidy, lying, &c. all the parts and knowledge in the world will never procure you esteem, friendship, or respect. A strange concurrence of circumstances has sometimes raised very bad men to high stations, but they have been raised like criminals to a pillory, where their persons and their crimes, by being more conspicuous, are only the more known, the more detested, and the more pelted and insulted."[10]

5. *Fix upon a high standard of action.*

Jackson subscribed to the timeless adage that actions speak louder than words. His adult life was highly regimented. One of his closest friends recalled: "Nothing but absolute illness ever caused him to relax his rigid system of rules: he would rise in the midst of the most animated conversation, like the very slave of the clock, as soon as his hour had struck, and go to his study. . . . His power of concentration was so great that he was able wholly to abstract himself from whatever was extraneous to the subject at hand."[11]

There were specific times for specific things: praying, teaching, drilling, reading, tending to his garden, exercising, relaxing with his wife. Seated idly and staring out the window were never characteristics of Jackson's daily schedule. No time existed for frivolities.

He had physical and mental energy; he regularly used them both. Jackson believed in physical fitness and aerobics decades before either became an art. To colleagues in both civilian and military life, Jackson seemed so indefatigable that when he appeared a bit weary, people thought him ill.

Life was a vehicle for accomplishment. Time was irreplaceable. Jackson therefore was brisk in everything he did. "Action is the proper fruit of knowledge," Thomas Fuller insisted. John Fletcher drew a simple analogy: "Great actions speak great minds." Thomas Huxley added: "The great end of life is not knowledge but action."

By the late spring of 1862, Jackson had become arguably the most famous field commander in the world. Two assessments by soldiers on opposite sides underlay the worldwide esteem that came to Jackson. His mapmaker, Maj. Jed Hotchkiss, observed:

"The last advice he always gave to any one sent to discharge a difficult task was: 'Never take counsel of your fears.'" Once all preparations had been made with painstaking care, Hotchkiss added, Jackson "went about his work with a persistency and with an abiding trust in Providence for securing success. . . . [He] believed with a boundless faith in the guiding and over-ruling Providence—a Providence that could only be met by all possible efforts on the part of him that would be benefited by such Providence."[12]

An officer in the Union army gave this opinion for Jackson's achievements: "His chief characteristics as a military leader were his quick perceptions of the weak points of the enemy, his ever readiness, the astounding rapidity of his movements, his sudden and unexpected onslaughts, and the persistency with which he followed them up. His ruling maxim was that war meant fighting, and fighting meant killing, and right loyally did he live up to it. . . . With him it was the voice of the Lord piloting him to the tents of the Midianites."[13]

It is man's highest interest not to violate or attempt to violate the rules which infinite wisdom has laid down.

Puritan poet Anne Bradstreet declared in 1664: "Authority without wisdom is like a heavy axe without an edge, fitter to bruise than polish."

In 1851, following his allegiance with the Lexington Presbyterian Church, the twenty-seven-year-old Jackson had two principal goals in life: He wanted to love God fully, and he wanted God to love him. His first resolution toward those objectives was a promise to himself never to "violate the known will of God." He never did.[14]

Jackson used a number of biblical verses to help him obey the "infinite wisdom" he sought to attain. Two examples were: "The fear of the Lord is the beginning of wisdom" (Psalm 111:10), and "Wisdom is the principal thing: therefore get wisdom: and with all thy getting get understanding" (Proverbs 4:7).

The means by which men are to attain great elevation may be classed in three great divisions: physical, mental & moral.

Whatever relates to health belongs to the first.

Whatever relates to improvement of the mind belongs to the second.

The formation of good manners & virtuous habits constitutes [the] third.

Here is clear evidence of how the orderly Jackson reduced life in all of its complexities to three simple premises.

It should not be surprising that attention to health was the first step toward improvement. Medical knowledge in the first half of the nineteenth century was not too distant from practices in the Middle Ages. Physicians of Jackson's time often relied on hand-me-down remedies and almanacs. Not one effective medicine existed for treating any disease or condition. With no effective remedy available for anything, people diagnosed themselves, created their own medicines, and engaged in self-treatment that did honor to the field of homeopathy.

Jackson suffered from a number of ills during the first half of his life. Whether he was or was not a hypochondriac is irrelevant. In his day he had a natural preoccupation with his health—largely because, like everyone else, he often did not feel well. His experiments and his dosages were sometimes superstitious, sometimes superfluous, but on occasion they were successful.

Perhaps Jackson was quirky about the supposed benefits of spas and metal-based drugs. Nevertheless, he actively sought relief with the same determination that he applied to other aspects of life. It proved profitable. Before his death, he was in far better physical condition than most of his contemporaries.

Improvement of the mind required greater exertion, but Jackson also succeeded there. "Knowledge," Lord Chesterfield wrote, "is a comfortable and necessary retreat and shelter for us in an advanced age; and if we do not plant it while young, it will give us no shade when we grow old. . . . If you should sometimes think [studying] a little laborious, consider, that labour is the unavoidable fatigue of a necessary journey. The more hours a day you travel, the sooner you will be at your journey's end. The sooner you qualify for your liberty, the sooner you shall have it."[15]

Midway through Jackson's Civil War career, one of his key staff officers received a surprise. "I was for a time doubtful as to Jackson's knowledge of general subjects from reading and observation, but after a few months of intimate relations with him in the camp, on the march and on the battlefield, I found that no matter what subject came up for conversation, comment or opinion, that he had at hand a store of general information such as could not have been acquired but by extensive reading and close observation."[16]

While seeking always to broaden his knowledge, Jackson worked in reverse to curtail any ambition. The pursuit of earthly gains ran the danger of provoking the wrath of God, he believed. Over and over he reminded himself that his real glory would come in heaven, not mortal life. As he once wrote his wife: "These [mortal] things are earthly and transitory. . . . My prayer is that such may ever be the feeling of my heart."[17]

Such devotion created a man so often locked within himself. Capt. Charles M. Blackford of the Second Virginia Cavalry noted in August 1862: "There is a magnetism in Jackson, but it is not personal. All admire his genius and great deeds; no one could love the man for himself. He seems to be cut off from his fellow-man and to commune with his own spirit only, or with spirits of which we know not."[18]

It was to curb such criticisms as those by Captain Blackford that Jackson labored constantly to acquire good manners and display virtuous habits. He was mindful of Lord Chesterfield's warning: "Manners . . . adorn and give an additional force and luster to both virtue and knowledge. They prepare and smooth the way for the progress of both; and are, I fear, with the bulk of mankind, more engaging than either. Remember the infinite advantage of manners; . . . good sense will suggest the great rules to you, good company will do the rest."[19]

As for the attainment of Jackson's third great means to the end of self-elevation—"the formation of good manners & virtuous habits," his book of maxims stands as a testament.

SECTION V

Politeness and Good Breeding[1]

I T IS GOOD-BREEDING alone," Lord Chesterfield wrote, "that can prepossess people in your favour at first sight, more time being necessary to discover greater talents. . . . I hardly know anything so difficult to attain, or so necessary to possess, as perfect good-breeding; which is equally inconsistent with a stiff formality, an impertinent forwardness, and an awkward bashfulness."[2]

Jackson could not erase his impoverished beginnings or his barren upbringing, but he could overcome them through an arduous campaign of self-improvement. Some of his first steppingstones were "politeness and good breeding." He equated politeness with courtesy. Good breeding had nothing to do with pedigree; Jackson used the two words to mean training in the art of good behavior.

From Lord Chesterfield, Jackson also learned the following: "Know that as learning, honour, and virtue are absolutely necessary to gain you the esteem and admiration of mankind; politeness and good-breeding are equally necessary to make you welcome and agreeable in conversation and common life. . . . A genteel manner prepossesses people in your favour, bends them toward you, and makes them wish to be like you."[3]

That Jackson was successful in these endeavors is undeniable. Drawbacks, however, were there as well. Jackson was not always uniformly kind; on occasion he was knowingly impolite. As a general, he had intolerance for officers who gave less than his own blind obedience to orders. Furthermore, Jackson never fully overcame the introverted nature implanted in childhood. James Power Smith of his staff asserted: "Jackson, himself a man of strong convictions and strong will . . . required obedience and expected efficient service. For the selfishly ambitious, for the self-indulgent, the idle and indifferent to duty, he had only rebuke, perhaps contempt." Smith continued: "There were cases of military discipline in which he seemed to be unjust and unrelenting. . . . No doubt he was sometimes mistaken; but this is certainly true, he bore no ill will to any one and put away as unworthy of him any thought of recrimination against those who made charges against him."[4]

Another aide noted: "The General always kept himself very much apart and, although he was uniformly polite to all persons who came to see him, he did not encourage social calls. He was especially considerate to young officers and privates when duties brought them into his presence."[5]

Good-breeding or true politeness is the art of showing men by external signs the internal regard we have for them.

Dr. Hunter McGuire, Jackson's personal physician during the Civil War, later noted: "As I look back on the two years that I was daily, indeed hourly, with him, his gentleness as a man, his great kindness, his tenderness to those in trouble and afflic-tion . . . impressed me more than his wonderful prowess as a great warrior."[6]

One of Jackson's author-counselors asserted: "In our search after quests . . . we should address ourselves first to the timid, the retiring, and especially to strangers. . . . The Christian should prove the impartiality of his benevolence . . . [and be] contented with enjoying the secret satisfaction of reflecting that perhaps he has entertained some angel unawares."[7]

Politeness and good breeding were absolutely necessary for adorning any talent, Lord Chesterfield believed. "The scholar without good-breeding is a pedant; the philosopher, a cynic; the soldier, a brute; and every man disagreeable."[8]

It arises from good sense improved by good company.

The roots of this maxim likely came from Lord Chesterfield's statement that good breeding was "the result of much good sense, some good-nature, and a little self-denial for the sake of others, and with a view to obtain the same indulgence from them."[9]

Good company and good manners, Izaak Walton observed, "are the very sinews of virtue." On the other hand, Lord Chesterfield stressed, "a man's own good-breeding is his best security against other people's ill-manners."[10]

In previous maxims, Jackson had so often emphasized the need for "good company" that his axiom here appears more as a reminder.

It must be acquired by practice and not by books.

Practice makes perfect, an old adage reasons. Jackson fully admitted that while he read much, the real value came from taking what one had learned and putting it into action.

He never ceased in trying to improve himself. In the early 1850s, when his efforts at self-betterment were in full bloom, Jackson urged his sister to let her children study in Lexington. "Without a good education they must ever fall short of that position in life which they ought to occupy."[11]

A few months later, he counseled a niece on spelling and grammar. "If a person commences reading before learning to spell well, he will not be apt to ever learn much about spelling; because reading is more pleasant than spelling . . . though I am now 36 years old, yet still I am mortified at my spelling words wrong. In writing this letter I have had to look in the Dictionary to see how a word was spelt, and so I expect it will be all my life."[12]

Jackson continued to have trouble with spelling—as is evident in several of his maxims.

His studies never ceased. In 1857, following his second marriage, Jackson and his wife began home life in Lexington. Anna's first letter to Jackson's beloved sister was cheerful and upbeat. The bride, however, could not conceal one disappointment. "He has been very busy since [our] return and is rather more studious than I would like him to be as I see nothing of him in his study hours."[13]

Be kind, condescending & affable.

A Presbyterian guide in Jackson's library contains the highlighted passage: "All mankind are members of one great family; and to get along pleasantly and peaceably with the world, we must be careful to observe the *law of kindness*. . . . One of your texts tells you not to prefer yourself (Rom. XII, 10), and there is another which I think I did not point out to you: 'Be courteous.'"[14]

Lord Chesterfield also had something to add to the subject. "The desire of pleasing is at least half the art of doing it: the rest depends only upon the manner; which attention, observation, and frequenting good company, will teach. But if you are lazy, careless, and indifferent whether you please or not, depend upon it you will never please."[15]

Jackson's friend, the Reverend James R. Graham, considered "marvelous self-control" to be one of Jackson's strongest qualities. "He possessed it in a degree I have never seen equaled. . . . Almost every one who knew him at all, can give some instance of his perfect mastery of himself under circumstances of trial." The Winchester minister closed this discussion with an appropriate biblical verse: "He that is slow to anger is better than the mighty, and he that ruleth his spirit than he that taketh a city."[16]

Any one who has any thing to say to a fellow [human] being to say it with kind feelings & a sincere desire to please & this when ever it is done will atone for much awkwardness in the manner of expression.

Jackson's favorite English tutor offered his son—and posterity—a number of precepts on the advantages of pleasurable company. "Vulgar, low expressions, awkward motions and addresses, vilify, as they imply either a very low turn of mind, or low education and low company. . . . Consider all of your circumstances seriously; and you will find that, of all arts, the art of pleasing is the most necessary for you to study and possess. . . . Most arts require long study and application; but the most useful art of all, that of pleasing, requires only the desire."[17]

As Jackson wrestled with his deep-seated reticence, he had to master a strong tendency toward silence. Yet his taciturnity persisted and seemed to grow more pronounced in the Civil War. A Louisiana artillery captain voiced a mixture of wonder and disgust when he once observed: "If silence is golden, then Jackson is rich indeed!"[18]

The best way Jackson overcame this "affliction" was to be a good listener. He consistently preferred saying a little while listening a lot.

Forced complaisance is fopping & affected easiness is ridiculous.

A favorite and marked thought in one of Jackson's books on civility was the statement: "There should be nothing in the conduct of the Christian unpleasing to the man of the world, unless it be his godliness."[19]

Another reminder for Jackson was this advice: "To be civil, and to be civil with ease (which is properly called good-breeding) is the only way to be beloved, and well received in company; that to be ill-bred, and rude, is intolerable, and the way to be kicked out of company; and that to be bashful, is to be ridiculous."[20]

Some men who profess faith, one author declared, "would have us distinctly understand that they are not 'man-pleasers.' They have attempted to please both God and man, but have learned that it is not possible to do both; and henceforth their one aim shall be how they please God."[21]

Jackson needed no reminder that following God's commandments was the paramount object of life. Foremost among those rules of conduct, to Jackson, was honesty. It was an obsession with him. His honesty was as rigid as his insistence on truth.

One afternoon Jackson and his wife Anna were walking when they passed an apple tree. Several apples had fallen to the ground. Anna asked her husband to step over the fence and get them a couple of apples. As they had fallen from the tree, no one would miss them.

In a kindly manner Jackson replied: "No, I do not think it would be right to do that. I am sure that Colonel R—— would have no objection, and would gladly give them to us if he were here, but I cannot take them without his leave."[22]

One day in the Shenandoah Valley, Jackson and an aide had been riding silently for an hour or two when the general suddenly turned and asked: "Did you ever think, sir, what an opportunity a battlefield affords liars?"[23]

Good breeding is opposed to selfishness, vanity or pride.

The sins of selfishness, vanity, and pride have drawn the scorn of countless writers throughout the ages.

Seventeenth-century epigrammatist François de la Rochefoucauld wrote of selfishness: "Virtues lose themselves in self-interest, as streams lose themselves in the sea." To Lord Chesterfield, "vanity is the more odious and shocking to everybody, because everybody, without exception, has vanity; and two vanities can never love one another."[24]

Alexander Pope underscored the dangers of pride with these lines: "Of all the causes which conspire to blind / Man's erring judgment, and misguide the mind, / What the weak head with strongest bias rules, / Is Pride, the never failing vice of fools."

These traits were not part of Jackson's makeup. His brother-in-law, caustic D. Harvey Hill, smiled often at how disarrayed Jackson became when compliments and strong attention came his way.[25] One of many Presbyterian minister-friends found Jackson "simple and unsophisticated in his manners. He did not seem to think himself a great man."[26]

Endeavor to please with out hardly allowing it to be perceived.

English poet Mathew Prior once preached: "If thou wouldst be happy, learn to please." Eighteenth-century British statesman George Lyttelton lauded any man who "pleased you by not studying to please."

Subsequent writers stressed the same theme. Jackson marked these words in one of his books: "There is no holy affection that either is not mingled with or does not subside in cheerfulness. Even disappointment, perplexity, and grief, those fatal disturbers of unbelieving minds, bring peace to the trusting soul and prepare it for unusual glory."[27]

Lord Chesterfield observed: "A cheerful, easy countenance and behaviour are very useful; they make fools think you are a good-natured man; and they make designing men think you are an undesigning one."[28]

By the spring of 1853, Jackson considered himself a worthy member of Lexington society. He told his sister: "I am invited to a large party to night, and among the scramble, expect to come in for my share of fun."[29] To one witness, Jackson's "resignation was very perfect, and to wear the aspect of cheerfulness became a fixed principle."[30]

Plain rules for attaining the character of a well bred man.

In his final four maxims, Jackson returned to the art of conversation. Each of the four had been stated or implied in the second section of quotations. The iteration here was almost natural, for learning to be comfortable when talking to people was one of the most difficult tasks he faced in the first three-fourths of his life. Behind much of the success Jackson achieved were his two wives and the several genuine friends he made in Lexington after his 1851 move to the Virginia Military Institute.

1. Never weary your company by talking too long or too frequently.

The Reverend Daniel Ewing, who came to know Jackson well during the war, commented: "In conversation he did not aspire to be a leader [and] contributed his part with unaffected modesty."[31]

A favorite story that circulated throughout the Confederacy was of a perturbed Jackson responding to numerous inquiries from the War Department with the terse message: "Send me more men, and fewer questions."[32]

2. *Always look people in the face when addressing them & generally when they address you.*

Lord Chesterfield, however, stated, "never hold any body by the button, or the hand, in order to be heard out; for, if people are not willing to hear you, you had much better hold your tongue than them."[33]

The fact that Jackson was so intense in everything he did ensured that when he spoke to you, he looked at you. Such intensity applied as well when he listened. After all, he reasoned, more knowledge came from what you received than from what you gave.

3. *Attend to a person who is addressing you.*

Simple courtesy demanded that one give attention to anyone who was trying to engage in conversation. Lord Chesterfield told his son: "If a man accosts you, and talks to you ever so dully or frivolously, it is worse than rudeness, it is brutality, to shew him, by a manifest inattention to what he says, that you think him a fool or a blockhead, and not worth hearing."[34]

4. Do not interrupt the person who is speaking by saying yes or no & such like at every sentence. An occasional assent either by word or action may be well enough.

"Good manners are made up of petty sacrifices," Ralph Waldo Emerson declared. The ancient philosopher Epictetus once gave this commentary on anatomy: "Nature has given to man one tongue, but two ears, that we may hear from others twice as much as we speak."

Jackson might not agree with a speaker, but that person rarely knew it. Margaret Preston was amazed at Jackson's demeanor in this regard. "No harsh judgments or incriminations were ever heard from his lips. Though most discriminating in his estimates of men, he was reticent to the last degree in passing judgment upon them. 'Judge not that ye be not judged,' he understood to be as positive a command as 'thou shalt not steal.' Yet he would say, 'It is quite contrary to my nature to keep silence when I cannot but disapprove. Indeed I may as well confess that it would often give me *real satisfaction* to express just what I feel, but this would be to disobey the divine precept, and I dare not do it.'"[35]

SECTION VI

Objects to Be Affected by Ellie's Death

lthough this brief section appears on the first page of the book of maxims, it was Jackson's final entry.

To eradicate ambition

To eradicate resentment

To produce humility

If you desire to be more heavenly minded, think more of the things of Heaven and less of the things of Earth.

Jackson was in full manhood when he first felt the emotion of romantic love. He became increasingly acquainted with Elinor Junkin, daughter of the Washington College president in Lexington. Before long, Jackson said to his friend, Prof. D. Harvey Hill: "I don't know what has changed me. I used to think her plain, but her face now seems to me all sweetness."

Hill laughed and replied: "You are in love; that's what is the matter!"

Jackson "blushed up to the eyes." He had never been in love before, he confessed, but he certainly "felt differently toward this lady from what he had ever felt before."[1]

The couple married in August 1853. Their marriage lasted only fourteen months. The sudden death of his first love was devastating for Jackson. It was two months before he could write a letter. Then he told an uncle that memories of Ellie were "sustaining me through the most trying of all earthly afflictions." Jackson reflected for a moment then added: "But what is life, it is but a span, it will soon be over, and I welcome its close. Yet while I am here, I know that all will be well."[2]

A few weeks later, he wrote Ellie's sister: "Though I have been speaking to you of the things of time, yet my personal interest in things here which affect myself, have much diminished. And I am looking forward with pleasure to that time when I shall only be seen by those who love me as I now see *Dear Ellie*."[3]

In that atmosphere of grief, Jackson put the book of maxims away. The little volume and its entries represented a vital, formative stage in his life—a stage that began with social uncertainty and ended with personal tragedy. Jackson persevered through it all, and in the end he was an infinitely better man for his efforts.

His resolve for self-improvement contains the same inspiration as his life as a Christian soldier. The determination of early manhood served him well in full manhood. His personal achievements in the early 1850s substantiated another of Lord Chesterfield's doctrines: "Aim at perfection in every thing, though in most things it is unattainable; however, they who aim at it, and persevere, will come much nearer it, than those whose laziness and despondency make them give it up as unattainable."[4]

EPILOGUE

THREE YEARS AFTER ELLIE'S death, Jackson remarried. His second wife was Mary Anna Morrison. Like Elinor Junkin, Anna was the daughter of a Presbyterian minister and college president. Her father was one of the founders of Davidson College in North Carolina. Anna was also bright, charming, and possessed of strong religious tenets. Jackson would spend the happiest six years of his life with Anna. Two children came of the union; one survived infancy.

Civil war traumatically interrupted this quiet life in Lexington. "War has no charms for me," Jackson told a friend. "I've seen too many of its horrors."[1] Nevertheless, when Virginia left the Union, Jackson's course of action was clear.

"His allegiance was to his state," Dr. Hunter McGuire explained. "He loved it better than his fame or life, better than everything else on the face of this earth save his own honor, and anything or anybody that impeded the establishment of her sovereignty would be swept aside if it was in his power."[2]

Jackson was convinced that the beliefs and activities of the federal government in the 1850s ran counter to those of the Founding Fathers in the 1780s. A central authority dominated by Northern radicals intended to deny the Southern states their sovereign rights. In Jackson's eyes, it was as if God had placed a curse on America. Therefore, the side that displayed the purest religious convictions would win the Civil War.

He went into the field to fight with Old Testament fury in order to attain New Testament faith. Hence his views of war and its necessities were as stern as those of Joshua, David, and Gideon of old. Early in the struggle, Jackson told his surgeon: "War means fighting. To fight is the duty of a soldier. March swiftly, strike the foe with all your strength, and take way from him everything you can. Injure him in every possible way, and do it quickly."[3]

Jackson became a familiar and beloved figure in the Confederate armies of Virginia. One of the best descriptions of "Old Jack," as his men called him, came from Dr. McGuire: "In person Jackson was a tall man, six feet high, angular, strong, with rather large feet and hands. He rather strided along as he walked, taking long steps and swinging his body a little. There was something firm and decided, however, even in his gait. His eyes were dark blue, large, and piercing. He looked straight at you and through you almost as he talked. His nose was aquiline, his nostrils thin and mobile. His mouth was broad, his lips very thin. Generally they were compressed. He spoke in terse, short sentences, always to the point. . . . His hair was brown and inclined to auburn. His beard was brown. He was as gentle and kind as a woman to those that he loved. There was sometimes a softness and tenderness about him that was very striking. Under every and all circumstances he never forgot that he was a Christian and acted up to his Christian faith unswervingly, and yet he was not a bigoted denominationalist."[4]

Within two years, Jackson's military accomplishments in the Civil War were so outstanding that he was the object of international renown. There was no pleasure in it for him. Anna Jackson told a reporter in the postwar years that "nothing but the loftiest sense of duty could have kept him amid scenes of carnage. His whole correspondence with me was full of expressed and implied horror of war and bloodshed. I am convinced that one of the reasons compelling him to the positive and vigorous course that he pursued was the knowledge that it must speedily release him from the repugnant work in which he was engaged. . . . Nothing but the most positive sense of deep religious duty could have nerved him to go through what he did."[5]

Suddenly he was gone. On May 2, 1863, in the chaos of the battle of Chancellorsville, Jackson was accidentally shot by his own men. The general died eight days later, and with him went many hopes for the Confederate cause.

Margaret Preston summarized well Jackson's feelings as a commander. "To serve his country, to do God's will, to make as short work as possible of the fearful struggle, to be ready for death if at any moment it should come to him—these were the uppermost ideals of his mind, and he would put aside, with an impatient expression, the words of confidence and praise that would be lavished upon him. 'Give God the glory' would be his curt reply."[6]

In a postwar Memorial Day address in Winchester, former congressman and Jackson confidant Alexander Boteler stated: "We remember how unselfishly he devoted himself to the cause he espoused; how successfully he defended it; how calmly he encountered dangers; how resolutely he overcame difficulties; how consistently he maintained his Christian character; and how singularly free he was from the ordinary frailties of humanity."[7]

Looking at Thomas Jackson's life from the broadest perspective gives a picture of the man as well as the general. He was one of the most brilliant military strategists and powerful field commanders in history. The military ingenuity was there, but so was the determination of a lonely orphan who made himself a learned gentleman welcome in every society.

One of the books in his library was a biography of the Tennessee soldier-president Andrew Jackson. Early in the book was a passage that Thomas Jackson liked well enough to mark in the margin. Jackson unknowingly highlighted his own epitaph. "He lived a hero, and died a Christian. He is gone from a world where he was recognized as among the greatest of men, to an immortal companionship with the greatest and purest of all the ages."[8]

NOTES

Introduction

1. Alexander Hunter, *Johnny Reb and Billy Yank* (New York, 1905), 365.

2. John H. Worsham, *One of Jackson's Foot Cavalry* (Jackson, Tenn., 1964), 102.

3. Catherine C. Hopley, *"Stonewall" Jackson, Late General of the Confederate States Army* (London, 1863), 177.

4. Mary Anna Jackson, *Life and Letters of General Thomas J. Jackson (Stonewall Jackson)* (New York, 1892), 30.

5. See James I. Robertson Jr., *Stonewall Jackson: The Man, The Soldier, The Legend* (New York, 1997), 22–26.

6. John C. Waugh, *The Class of 1846* (New York, 1994), 24.

7. John C. Tidball Memoir, Tidball Papers, U.S. Military Academy.

8. Thomas J. Jackson to Laura J. Arnold, March 23, 1848, Thomas J. Jackson Papers, Virginia Military Institute.

9. Lord Chesterfield, *Works of Lord Chesterfield, Including His Letters to His Son, & To Which Is Prefixed, An Original Life of the Author* (New York, 1838), 413, 482. Cited hereafter as Chesterfield, *Letters*.

10. Ibid., 31.

11. Thomas J. Jackson to Samuel L. Hays, February 2, 1849, Thomas J. Jackson Papers, Library of Congress.

12. Thomas J. Jackson to Laura J. Arnold, August 10, 1850, Jackson Papers, Library of Congress.

13. Jacob Abbott, *History of Cleopatra, Queen of Egypt* (New York, 1851), viii.

14. Charles Royster, *The Destructive War* (New York, 1991), 51.

15. For the incidents relating to Jackson's appointment to the VMI faculty, see Robertson, *Stonewall Jackson,* 99–104.

16. Philip B. Power, *"I Will:" Being the Determination of the Man of God* (New York, 1864), 12.

17. William B. Taliaferro, "Reminiscences of Jackson," William B. Taliaferro Papers, College of William and Mary. A Lexington student declared that cadets "feared [Jackson] in the lecture room, they paid the strictest deference to him on parade, but in showing a stranger the sights about the Institute, a cadet was never known to point out 'Old Jack' as one of the ornaments of the institution" (*Lexington Gazette,* September 4, 1928).

18. Anna Jackson, *Jackson,* 53.

19. Raleigh Edward Colston Reminiscences, University of North Carolina; *Southern Historical Society Papers* 43 (1920): 59.

20. George Junkin, *The Progress of the Age: An Address to the Literary Societies of Washington College* (Philadelphia, 1851), 11.

21. Clement D. Fishburne to Paul B. Barringer, April 16, 1903, Thomas J. Jackson File, Presbyterian Church (USA) Archives.

22. Robertson, *Stonewall Jackson,* 130.

23. Clement D. Fishburne Memoirs, University of Virginia.

24. *Century Magazine* 32 (1886): 933.

25. *Southern Historical Society Papers* 6 (1878): 265.

26. George Winfred Hervey, *The Principles of Courtesy, with Hints and Observations on Manners and Courtesy* (New York, 1856), 288.

27. *Century Magazine* 47 (1893–94): 626; Colston Reminiscences. According to an early biographer, Jackson's first effort before the society was so embarrassing that he halted in the middle of the presentation and sat down. "As predicted by his friends, he did not stay down long, but rising to his feet began again and

repeated this programme until he learned to declaim. . . . No one laughed at him. He was too soundly respected for fun making." William C. Chase, *Story of Stonewall Jackson* (Atlanta, 1901), 177.

28. *Century Magazine* 32 (1886): 927.

29. Colston Reminiscences.

30. Thomas J. Arnold, *Early Life and Letters of General Thomas J. Jackson* (New York, 1916), 194.

31. For the effects of these two compilations on American society in general and Jackson in particular, see Christopher R. Lawton, *The Pilgrim's Progress: Thomas J. Jackson's Journey Towards Civility and Citizenship* (Lexington, Va., 2001), 7–9, 28–30.

32. Chesterfield, *Letters*, 144.

33. Jackson's library of 122 volumes is at the Virginia Historical Society. The majority of volumes range in subject matter from history and biography to military texts, studies relating to optics, and religious works. A few volumes treat of civility, and a small number are books that Anna Jackson added to the collection.

34. Elizabeth Preston Allan, *The Life and Letters of Margaret Junkin Preston* (Boston, 1903), 61–62.

35. Thomas J. Jackson to Laura J. Arnold, November 14, 1854, Jackson Papers, VMI; Allan, *Margaret Junkin Preston*, 72.

36. Arnold, *Early Life and Letters*, 14.

37. Chesterfield, *Letters* 127; Thomas J. Jackson to Laura J. Arnold, February 28, 1848, Jackson Papers, VMI. Christopher Lawton developed the three parallels given here in *The Pilgrim's Progress*, 28–29.

38. Chesterfield, *Letters*, 13; Thomas J. Jackson to Laura J. Arnold, March 23, 1848, Jackson Papers, VMI.

39. Chesterfield, *Letters*, 31; Thomas J. Jackson to Samuel L. Hays, February 2, 1849, Jackson Papers, Library of Congress. The study specifically cited by Lord Chesterfield and Jackson was Charles Rollin, *Ancient History of the Egyptians, Carthaginians, Assyrians, Babylonians, Medes and Persians, Grecians and Macedonians*, 8 vols. (New York, 1843–44).

Section I: Choice of Friends

1. Alexander H. Wiggins, "The Mysteries of Nature," in *The Christian Keepsake and Missionary Manual for 1849* (Philadelphia, 1849), 194.
2. Chesterfield, *Letters*, 321.
3. Ibid., 136.
4. *Southern Historical Society Papers* 35 (1907): 83; Robertson, *Stonewall Jackson*, 220, 342.
5. George Washington to Bushrod Washington, January 15, 1783, *The Writings of George Washington* (Washington, 1938), 26:39–40.
6. Chesterfield, *Letters*, 159.
7. Hervey, *Principles of Courtesy*, 308.
8. Anna Jackson, *Jackson*, 47, 70.
9. Chesterfield, *Letters*, 159. See also idem, 220, 342.
10. See Robertson, *Stonewall Jackson*, 136–37, 145, 181, 205–6.
11. Chesterfield, *Letters*, 132–33, 621.
12. Ibid., 159. In the seventeenth century, English poet Abraham Cowley mused in *Of Myself*: "Acquaintance I would have, but when 't depends / Not on the number, but the choice of friends."
13. Arnold, *Early Life and Letters*, 20.
14. Chesterfield, *Letters*, 93.
15. Hervey, *Principles of Courtesy*, 294.
16. Chesterfield, *Letters*, 620.

Section II: Rules of Conversation

1. Lord Chesterfield, *Letters*, 174–75, 308.
2. Ibid., 457–58.
3. Ibid., 161.
4. Hervey, *Principles of Courtesy*, 296.
5. Robert L. Dabney, *Life and Campaigns of Lieut.-Gen. Thomas J. Jackson (Stonewall Jackson)* (Richmond, 1866), 79–80.
6. Chesterfield, *Letters*, 190, 619.

7. *Southern Historical Society Papers* 19 (1891): 314–15.

8. McHenry Howard, *Recollections of a Maryland Confederate and Staff Officer Under Johnston, Jackson and Lee* (Baltimore, 1914), 181; Robertson, *Stonewall Jackson,* 587.

9. Chesterfield, *Letters,* 145, 318. The Englishman wrote in an earlier letter to his son: "Want of attention about what is [transpiring] makes man so like either a fool or a madman, that, for my part, I see no real difference. A fool never has thought; a madman has lost it; and an absent man is, for the time, without it." Idem, 100.

10. Dabney, *Jackson,* 80.

11. Chesterfield, *Letters,* 223.

12. Dabney, *Jackson,* 77.

13. *Century Magazine* 32 (1886): 927–28.

14. *Seventy Times Seven, or, The Law of Kindness* (Philadelphia, 1857), 66.

15. Chesterfield, *Letters,* 160. The Englishman also advised his son: "Avoid as much as you can, in mixed companies, argumentative, polemical conversations; which, though they should not, yet certainly do indispose . . . the contending parties towards each other." Idem, 223.

16. Ibid., 145.

17. Ibid., 160, 223.

18. Hervey, *Principles of Courtesy,* 224.

19. Chesterfield, *Letters,* 94.

20. Robertson, *Stonewall Jackson,* 138.

21. Chesterfield, *Letters,* 458.

22. *Century Magazine* 32 (1886): 928.

23. *Rockbridge County News,* January 24, 1935.

24. *Century Magazine* 32 (1886): 929.

25. Chesterfield, *Letters,* 223, 227.

26. Dabney H. Maury, *Recollections of a Virginian in the Mexican, Indian, and Civil Wars* (New York, 1894), 71–72. See also Robertson, *Stonewall Jackson,* 311, 321, 349–50, 452, 627–28, 678–80.

27. *Century Magazine* 32 (1886), 927.

28. Chesterfield, *Letters*, 70–71. See also idem, 341.

29. William Spottswood White Narrative, Charles W. Dabney Papers, University of North Carolina.

30. Hervey, *Principles of Courtesy*, 50.

Section III: Guides for Good Behavior

1. *Southern Historical Society Papers* 25 (1897): 104.

2. Quoted in Royster, *The Destructive War*, 56.

3. Hervey, *Principles of Courtesy*, 27–28.

4. Anna Jackson, *Jackson*, 45.

5. Taliaferro, "Reminiscences of Jackson."

6. Dabney, *Jackson*, 87; *Index* (London), June 4, 1863.

7. Henry Kyd Douglas, *I Rode with Stonewall* (Chapel Hill, 1940), 217.

8. Hervey, *Principles of Courtesy*, xiv, xxii.

9. Chesterfield, *Letters*, 279.

10. Colston Reminiscences.

11. *Southern Historical Society Papers* 19 (1891): 311–12; 25 (1897), 106. A typical bland reaction by Jackson to humor is in Robertson, *Stonewall Jackson*, 629–30.

12. Chesterfield, *Letters*, 179–80. See also idem, 419.

13. *The Collected Works of Abraham Lincoln* (New Brunswick, N.J., 1953), 3:424; 4:9.

14. William B. Hesseltine, *Ulysses S. Grant, Politician* (New York, 1938), 384.

15. Jedediah Hotchkiss Journal, August 17, 1862, Hotchkiss Papers, Library of Congress.

16. W. H. C. Whiting to Robert L. Dabney, November 30, 1863, Dabney Papers.

17. *Century Magazine* 32 (1886): 929.

18. Sarah J. Hale, "Woodbine Cottage," in *Christian Keepsake*, 34–35.

19. Jedediah Hotchkiss to William C. Chase, March 28, 1892, Hotchkiss Papers.

20. Anna Jackson, *Jackson*, 70.

21. Arnold, *Early Life and Letters*, 312.

22. Ibid., 67.

23. Chesterfield, *Letters*, 627.

24. James R. Graham, "Some Reminiscences of Stonewall Jackson," *Winchester-Frederick County Historical Society Journal* 9 (1998–99): 97–98.

25. Thomas J. Jackson to Anna Jackson, August 5, 1861, Dabney Papers. Jackson's quotation was a reference to his favorite biblical verse, Romans 8:28.

26. Hopley, *Jackson*, 9.

27. Chesterfield, *Letters*, 49, 119. For an instance of Jackson's returning a book to the library in a driving rainstorm because he promised to have the volume back within an hour, see Robertson, *Stonewall Jackson*, 131.

28 *Century Magazine* 32 (1886): 933.

29. Robert L. Dabney notes, Dabney Papers.

30. Douglas, *I Rode with Stonewall*, 122.

31. Colston Reminiscences.

32. Robert U. Johnson and Clarence C. Buel, eds., *Battles and Leaders of the Civil War* (New York, 1884–87), 1:122.

33. *Index* (London), June 4, 1863.

34. William W. Blackford, *War Years with Jeb Stuart* (New York, 1945), 81.

35. Douglas, *I Rode with Stonewall*, 186. For incidents of Jackson's campaign with liquor, see Robertson, *Stonewall Jackson*, 230–31, 328, 418, 842.

36. Robertson, *Stonewall Jackson*, 246.

37. Ibid., 456.

38. *Century Magazine* 32 (1886): 933–34.

39. Chesterfield, *Letters*, 518.

40. Ibid., 519.

41. *Century Magazine* 32 (1886): 930.

42. Hervey, *Principles of Courtesy*, 58.

43. Chesterfield, *Letters*, 240.

44. *Life of Andrew Jackson, Embracing Anecdotes Illustrative of His Character* (Philadelphia, 1845), 120

45. Chesterfield, *Letters*, 21. See also idem, 174, 433, 519.

46. Hervey, *Principles of Courtesy*, 89–91.

47. Douglas, *I Rode with Stonewall*, 214.

48. Dabney, *Jackson*, 736. A similar opinion, by Jackson's mapmaker, Jedediah Hotchkiss, is in his March 28, 1892, letter to biographer William L. Chase. Hotchkiss Papers.

49. Chesterfield, *Letters*, 256–57.

50. Anna Jackson, *Jackson*, 65.

51. Arnold, *Early Life and Letters*, 312.

52. *Southern Historical Society Papers* 25 (1897): 99.

53. Robert L. Dabney to Goupil & Co., December 20, 1867, Henry Woodhouse Collection, R. W. Norton Art Gallery, Shreveport, La.

54. Susan L. Blackford, comp., *Letters from Lee's Army* (New York, 1947), 118.

55. Anna Jackson, *Jackson*, 69.

56. Dabney, *Jackson*, 71.

57. Hervey, *Principles of Courtesy*, 27–28, 34.

58. *Century Magazine* 46 (1893–94): 627–28.

59. Royster, *The Destructive War*, 60.

60. Arnold, *Early Life and Letters*, 66.

61. Anna Jackson, *Jackson*, 81. See also idem, 38, 72.

62. Dabney, *Jackson*, 63.

Section IV: Motives to Action

1. Graham, "Some Reminiscences," 82–83.

2. Joel Parker, *Invitations to True Happiness, and Motives for Becoming a Christian* (New York, 1844), 10, 134.

3. Thomas J. Jackson to Laura J. Arnold, April 2, 1851, Jackson Papers, Library of Congress.

4. Anna Jackson, *Jackson*, 105.

5. Ibid., 107–8.

6. Allan, *Margaret Junkin Preston*, 85–86.

7. Chesterfield, *Letters*, 374.

8. Chase, *Story of Stonewall Jackson*, 138–39.

9. Douglas, *I Rode with Stonewall*, 237.

10. Chesterfield, *Letters*, 316.

11. Allan, *Margaret Junkin Preston*, 76.

12. Jedediah Hotchkiss to William L. Chase, March 28, 1892, Hotchkiss Papers.

13. Tidball Memoir.

14. Robertson, *Stonewall Jackson*, 135.

15. Chesterfield, *Letters*, 166–67.

16. Jedediah Hotchkiss to William L. Chase, March 28, 1892, Hotchkiss Papers.

17. Anna Jackson, *Jackson*, 363–64.

18. Susan Leigh Blackford, comp., *Memoirs of Life In and Out of the Army in Virginia* (Lynchburg, Va., 1996), 1:185.

19. Chesterfield, *Letters*, 191.

Section V: Politeness and Good Breeding

1. According to Anna Jackson, her husband copied the ideas in this section from a book on etiquette entitled *Politeness and Good-breeding*. Anna Jackson, *Jackson*, 37–38.

2. Chesterfield, *Letters*, 127.

3. Ibid., 94, 99.

4. *Southern Historical Society Papers* 43 (1920): 65, 80.

5. Douglas, *I Rode with Stonewall*, 39–40.

6. *Southern Historical Society Papers* 25 (1897): 106.

7. Hervey, *Principles of Courtesy*, 50.

8. Chesterfield, *Letters*, 160.

9. Ibid., 288.

10. Ibid., 622.

11. Arnold, *Early Life and Letters*, 216.
12. Thomas J. Jackson to Grace Arnold, February 25, 1860, Jackson Papers, Library of Congress.
13. Robertson, *Stonewall Jackson*, 179.
14. *Seventy Times Seven*, 43.
15. Chesterfield, *Letters*, 141.
16. Graham, "Some Reminiscences," 88, 90. The biblical quotation is Proverbs 16:32.
17. Chesterfield, *Letters*, 267, 454, 622.
18. Charles W. Squires, "Autobiography," Library of Congress.
19. Hervey, *Principles of Courtesy*, 288.
20. Chesterfield, *Letters*, 95.
21. Hervey, *Principles of Courtesy*, 287.
22. Anna Jackson, *Jackson*, 69.
23. Robertson, *Stonewall Jackson*, x.
24. Chesterfield, *Letters*, 591.
25. *Century Magazine* 47 (1893–94): 627.
26. Robertson, *Stonewall Jackson*, 460.
27. Hervey, *Principles of Courtesy*, 45.
28. Chesterfield, *Letters*, 621.
29. Thomas J. Jackson to Laura J. Arnold, April 15, 1853, Jackson Papers, VMI.
30. Allan, *Margaret Junkin Preston*, 77.
31. Robertson, *Stonewall Jackson*, 460.
32. *Jefferson Davis and "Stonewall" Jackson* (Philadelphia, 1866), 263.
33. Chesterfield, *Letters*, 223.
34. Ibid., 289.
35. Allan, *Margaret Junkin Preston*, 83.

Section VI: Objects to Be Affected by Ellie's Death

1. *Century Magazine* 47 (1893–94): 627.
2. Thomas J. Jackson to Alfred Neale, January 3, 1855, Jackson File, U.S. Military Academy.

3. Thomas J. Jackson to Margaret Junkin, March 1, 1855, Margaret Junkin Preston Papers, University of North Carolina.

4. Chesterfield, *Letters*, 343.

Epilogue

1. Robertson, *Stonewall Jackson*, 320.

2. *Southern Historical Society Papers* 19 (1891): 310.

3. Ibid., 25 (1897): 104.

4. Ibid., 19 (1891): 302.

5. *Philadelphia Weekly Times*, April 7, 1877.

6. *Century Magazine* 32 (1886): 935.

7. Alexander Robinson Boteler Papers, Duke University.

8. *Life of Andrew Jackson*, 4.

WORKS CITED

Abbott, Jacob. *History of Cleopatra, Queen of Egypt.* New York: Harper & Bros., 1851.

Allan, Elizabeth Preston. *The Life and Letters of Margaret Junkin Preston.* Boston: Houghton, Mifflin and Co., 1903.

Arnold, Thomas J. *Early Life and Letters of General Thomas J. Jackson.* New York: Fleming H. Revell Co., 1916.

Bartlett, John. *Familiar Quotations: A Collection of Passages, Phrases, and Proverbs Traced to Their Sources in Ancient and Modern Literature.* Boston: Little, Brown and Co., 1992.

Blackford, Susan L., comp. *Letters from Lee's Army.* New York: Charles Scribner's Sons, 1947

————. *Memoirs of Life In and Out of the Army in Virginia.* 2 vols. Lynchburg, Va.: Warwick House Publishing, 1996.

Blackford, William W. *War Years with Jeb Stuart.* New York: Charles Scribner's Sons, 1945.

Boteler, Alexander Robinson. Papers. Duke University.

Century Magazine 1886, 1893–94.

Chase, William L. *Story of Stonewall Jackson.* Atlanta: D. E. Luther Publishing Co., 1901.

Chesterfield, Philip D. S. *Works of Lord Chesterfield, Including His Letters to His Son, & To Which Is Prefixed, An Original Life of the Author.* New York: Harper & Bros., 1838.

The Christian Keepsake, and Missionary Manual for MDCCCXLIX. Philadelphia: Brower, Hayes & Co., 1849.

Colston, Raleigh Edward. Reminiscences. University of North Carolina.

Dabney, Charles William. Papers. University of North Carolina.

Dabney, Robert Lewis. Letter. R. W. Norton Art Gallery, Shreveport, La.

————. *Life and Campaigns of Lieut.-Gen. Thomas J. Jackson, (Stonewall Jackson).* New York: Blelock & Co., 1866.

Douglas, Henry Kyd. *I Rode with Stonewall.* Chapel Hill: University of North Carolina Press, 1940.

Fishburne, Clement. Memoirs. University of Virginia.

Graham, James R. "Some Reminiscences of Stonewall Jackson." *Winchester-Frederick County Historical Society Journal,* 1998–99.

Hervey, George Winfred. *The Principles of Courtesy; With Hints and Observations on Manners and Habits.* New York: Harper & Bros., 1856.

Hesseltine, William B. *Ulysses S. Grant, President.* New York: Dodd, Mead & Co., 1938.

Hopley, Catherine C. *"Stonewall" Jackson, Late General of the Confederate States Army.* London: Chapman and Hall, 1863.

Hotchkiss, Jedediah. Papers. Library of Congress.

Howard, McHenry. *Recollections of a Maryland Confederate and Staff Officer under Johnston, Jackson, and Lee.* Baltimore: Williams & Wilkins, 1914.

Hunter, Alexander. *Johnny Reb and Billy Yank.* New York: The Neale Co., 1905.

Index (London), 1863.

Jackson, Mary Anna. *Life and Letters of General Thomas J. Jackson (Stonewall Jackson).* New York: Harper & Bros., 1892.

Jackson, Thomas Jackson. Book of Maxims. George and Catherine Davis Collection, Tulane University.

————. File. Presbyterian Church (USA) Archives.

————. Papers. Library of Congress.

————. Papers. Virginia Military Institute.

Jefferson Davis and "Stonewall" Jackson. Philadelphia: John E. Potter and Co., 1866.

Johnson, Robert U., and Clarence C. Buel, eds. *Battles and Leaders of the Civil War.* 4 vols. New York: The Century Co., 1887–88.

Junkin, George. *The Progress of the Age: An Address to the Literary Societies of Washington College.* Philadelphia: Published for the Societies, 1851.

Lawton, Christopher R. *The Pilgrim's Progress: Thomas J. Jackson's Journey Towards Civility and Citizenship.* Lexington, Va.: The Stonewall Jackson House, 2001.

Life of Andrew Jackson, Embracing Anecdotes Illustrative of His Character. Philadelphia: Lindsay & Blackiston, 1845.

Lincoln, Abraham. *The Collected Works of Abraham Lincoln.* 9 vols. New Brunswick, N.J.: Rutgers University Press, 1953–55.

Lexington Gazette, 1928.

Maury, Dabney H. *Recollections of a Virginian in the Mexican, Indian, and Civil Wars.* New York: C. Scribner's Sons, 1894.

Parker, Joel. *Invitations to True Happiness, and Motives for Becoming a Christian.* New York: Harper & Bros., 1844.

Philadelphia Weekly Times, 1877.

Power, Philip B. *"I Will": Being a Determination of the Man of God.* New York: Robert Carter & Brothers, 1864.

Preston, Margaret Junkin. Papers. University of North Carolina.

Robertson, James I., Jr. *Stonewall Jackson: The Man, The Soldier, The Legend.* New York: Macmillan Publishing USA, 1997.

Rockbridge County News, 1935.

Royster, Charles. *The Destructive War.* New York: Alfred A. Knopf, 1991.

Seventy Times Seven, or, The Law of Kindness. Philadelphia: Presbyterian Board of Publications, 1857.

Southern Historical Society Papers. 52 vols. Richmond: Southern Historical Society, 1876–1952.

Squires, Charles W. "Autobiography." Library of Congress.

Stevenson, Burton, ed. *The Home Book of Quotations Classical and Modern.* New York: Dodd, Mead & Company, 1958.

Taliaferro, William B. "Reminiscences of Jackson." William Booth Taliaferro Papers, College of William and Mary.

Tidball, John Caldwell. Memoir. U.S. Military Academy.

Washington, George. *The Writings of George Washington*. 39 vols. Washington: Government Printing Office, 1931–44.

Waugh, John C. *The Class of 1846*. New York: Warner Books, 1994.

Worsham, John H. *One of Jackson's Foot Cavalry*. Jackson, Tenn.: McCowat-Mercer Press, 1964.

INDEX